Managing Anger
in the Workplace

Donald Gibson, Ph.D.
& Bruce Tulgan

HRD PRESS
Amherst, Massachusetts

Published by: HRD Press, Inc.
                 22 Amherst Road
                 Amherst, MA 01002
                 800-822-2801 (U.S. and Canada)
                 413-253-3488
                 413-253-3490 (fax)
                 http://www.hrdpress.com

ISBN: 0-87425-677-1

Printed in Canada

Cover design by Eileen Klockars
Editorial and production services by Mary George

❦

*From Don: To my wife, Kathleen, and
our three inspired and inspiring children,
Nora, Abigail, and Nathan*

*From Bruce: To all those who have suffered
as a result of poorly managed anger
in the workplace*

Table of Contents

Acknowledgments

FIRST AND FOREMOST, we must thank the many thousands of incredible people who, over the years, have shared the lessons of their workplace experiences with RainmakerThinking. We also are grateful to all the business leaders and managers who have expressed so much confidence in our work at RainmakerThinking; thank you for giving us the opportunity to learn from the real management issues you deal with and solve on a daily basis. And to the tens of thousands who have attended our seminars, thanks for listening, for laughing, for sharing the wisdom of your experience, for pushing us with the really tough questions, for all of your kindness, and for continually teaching us.

Donald wishes to acknowledge the research colleagues who enhanced and excited his interest in the study of anger in the workplace. He is especially grateful to Sigal Barsade of Yale University, an unfailing friend, critic, and colleague who saw potential in this work; the Academy of Management Research Incubator, particularly Maurice Schweitzer, Ronda Callister, Joo Seng Tan, Barbara Gray, and Martin Davidson, who focused and challenged his thinking about anger; and

Art Swersey, Lisa Barron, Chris McCuster, and the many others who listened when he needed to vent.

We are also indebted to the many managers who participated in our interview and survey research for this book; thank you for giving so selflessly of your time and personal experience.

Many thanks as well to our friend and publisher, Bob Carkhuff, and his team at HRD Press; and to all our colleagues, present and past, at RainmakerThinking.

Finally, for our families and friends, we reserve our deepest and utmost gratitude.

Introduction

ANGER IS a fundamental human emotion, common to everyone's experience. It stems from our instinct for self-preservation and is both physiological and cognitive in nature. Many things can stimulate anger, and virtually all of us feel and express this emotion at some time in the different areas of our lives.

The typical workplace is particularly conducive to anger. Here we find complex relationships, chronic pressure, high stakes, and many factors beyond our control. These generate frustration, conflict, and anxiety—common causes of anger. We are all familiar with high-profile cases of workplace violence, and surely a burning issue for managers is figuring out how to prevent extreme outbursts that may result in injury or worse. But the more comprehensive task for managers and business leaders is to understand anger and learn how to handle it in all its workplace manifestations.

The Key to Anger Management

When we think about managing anger, we tend to think about controlling people who "over-express" their anger by behaving aggressively. However, an equally important problem is the "under-expression" of anger, when for one reason or another people do not show their anger. Both over- and under-expression lead to significant costs for individuals, teams, and organizations, and both must be dealt with effectively.

The key to managing anger, then, is *creating conditions in which anger can be expressed appropriately and productively.* This key reflects the underlying assumption of our pocket guide: that while anger can produce very damaging results, it is not necessarily a negative emotion. Indeed, anger can be a source of important data that should be recognized, processed, and acted upon. When effectively managed, anger can produce many positive results.

Overview of the Pocket Guide

The explanations, analyses, and best practices in this book come directly from two sources: ongoing workplace research conducted by RainmakerThinking since the mid 1990s, and academic research conducted by Donald Gibson while on the faculties of the Yale School of Management and Fairfield University. Here is a brief summary of the material covered:

> ➤ **Chapter 1: Anger in the Workplace.** We begin by outlining the basic components of anger and explaining the factors that contribute to anger in the workplace.

➤ **Chapter 2: The Costs of Anger in the Workplace.** Here we discuss the long- and short-term consequences of poorly managed anger and their meaning for individuals, work teams, and organizations.

➤ **Chapter 3: The Benefits of Anger in the Workplace.** This chapter focuses on the value of anger as a motivator and the value of the data provided by anger.

➤ **Chapter 4: Diagnosing Anger.** Here we lay out the signs and symptoms of anger along with guidelines for identifying anger, a skill especially important in the case of under-expressed anger. We also lay out some common anger syndromes that afflict many workplaces.

➤ **Chapter 5: Focus on the Source.** This chapter outlines the primary sources of workplace anger and offers guidelines for handling them. Also included are several case examples with brainstorming exercises that will help you practice the critical step of looking for underlying causes.

➤ **Chapter 6: Dealing With Your Own Anger.** Before you can effectively manage anger in others, you must be able to manage anger in yourself. Here you will find a six-step process for self-therapy that you can also use when coaching others on anger management.

➤ **Chapter 7: Dealing With the Angry Individual.**
You cannot take responsibility for the anger
of every person you work with, but you are
responsible for dealing with the anger of your
direct reports. The five-step intervention process in this chapter will help you do so.

➤ **Chapter 8: Dealing With Anger in Your
Organization or Team.** We focus here on the
problem of systemic causes and pervasive
anger. We discuss the elements of organizational culture that contribute to pervasive anger as well as those that diminish its likelihood.
We also provide a three-step intervention for
teams in crisis, and outline best practices for
organization-wide anger management.

Throughout this book, we've included:

- Clear and simple explanations based on real
workplace case studies

- Concrete action steps

- Room for brainstorming exercises

- Worksheets for applying the explanations and
action steps to the issues you are facing (or
may face) in your working life

It is our great hope that this material will help you
better understand anger in the workplace and more
effectively manage anger in yourself and others.

If the ideas and strategies in these pages help you improve your working life and add to your success, then we have succeeded with this pocket guide. Please let us know—we'd love to hear from you. Contact us at www.rainmakerthinking.com.

CHAPTER 1

Anger in the Workplace

THIS MORNING Mary got up on the wrong side of the bed. She had slept restlessly, consumed by worries about a presentation she had agreed to deliver today. "I shouldn't have to give this presentation," she kept thinking. "It's not even my project. Why did I agree to do it, anyway?" Long past dawn, she finally peered at the clock—and bolted from bed. Yet again her husband, an early riser, had forgotten to reset the alarm. "*Grrrr* . . . He'll be sorry when I get through with him," she said, throwing on her clothes. "No time for coffee, no time for breakfast," she grumbled, rushing out the door. "No time, no time! Late, late, late!"

Into the car Mary hopped, and off she raced . . . straight into a traffic jam. As she inched along, her frustration grew worse and worse. Patience was the only solution; still, Mary kept trying to switch lanes, and when a space opened up in the breakdown lane, she went for it. "Other people do it all the time," she assured herself.

The next thing Mary knew, she was handing a state trooper her license and registration. "I'm sorry, officer," she said, "I'm just in a big hurry. I'm running late." He was unimpressed. "Everyone here would like to drive in the breakdown lane. But I suppose you're special, right?" Mary said nothing. After an agonizing five-minute wait, the officer handed back her license and registration, along with a fifty-dollar ticket.

Now Mary was really late. So late, in fact, that the lot where she usually parked was full. By the time she found a parking spot, hiked the extra distance to her building, and made it to her office, she was in no mood for the nasty-toned voice mail her boss had left for her. "Mary, where are you?" he wanted to know. "It's nine-thirty. I'd better hear from you by ten o'clock!" She took a deep breath and headed for the ladies' room to collect herself before dealing with the rest of her day.

On her way out the office door, John, her assistant, came walking swiftly in her direction. "Mary," he said, "Can you wait a second? I need to ask you something." Mary stopped, fixed her eyes on him, and replied in a frightfully loud, stern voice, *"Not now, John! Why are you always in my way?"*

What Is Anger?

We've all dealt with angry people in our personal and professional lives. And we all know how it feels to be angry. But what exactly is anger?

Anger is a normal, basic emotion that ranges from mild irritation to intense rage. Like fear, anger stems from our instinct for self-preservation and is always provoked by some stimulus. The stimulus may be internal or external, direct or indirect. Common anger stimuli include betrayal, disapproval, deprivation, exploitation, frustration, humiliation, manipulation, restriction, and threat. In response to one or more of these triggering stimuli, the body releases two hormones, adrenaline and noradrenalin, which produce physiological arousal, including muscle tension, increased blood pressure, accelerated heart rate, and rapid breathing. That's why angry people often scowl, grind their teeth, shudder, glare, clench their fists, flush (or pale), and twitch.

But the effects of anger go way beyond these physical manifestations. Anger has a huge impact on our perceptions, interpretations, thinking, communication, and behavior. That's why angry people often have a difficult time listening to "reason" (or appreciating the "other side of the story"); speak in a cold monotone voice; yell; say things that are intimidating, threatening, or hurtful; and lash out physically at inanimate objects or, even worse, at animals or other people.

Of course, some people do not directly express their anger at all. They might try to deny and repress their feelings, which leaves the anger seething beneath the surface. Such unexpressed anger may find another outlet, such as physical symptoms. Or the unexpressed anger may come out in passive-aggressive forms, such as withdrawal from the relationship, disrespect, sarcasm, or lack of cooperation. Sometimes anger may go unexpressed until it emerges in an outburst, or until it's inadvertently redirected toward an individual, group, institution, or condition that is entirely unrelated to the true source of the anger.

In rare cases, individuals truly learn how to calm their anger internally until the feelings subside without ever being expressed. Of course, this response is healthier than over-expressing or repressing anger, but it doesn't tap into the potential benefits of anger.

It is critical to recognize that anger is not necessarily a negative emotion. Anger often signals important data about relationships, resources, circumstances, or procedures that need improvement. When that data is recognized, processed, and acted upon, anger can lead to productive actions and positive outcomes. Effectively managed, it can give us the strength to persist in our goals, confront competitors, generate new ideas, or approach colleagues and superiors with problems.

Anger in the Workplace

Anger is a challenging emotion to deal with in any context, but it is especially challenging in the workplace.

Why? Because there we tend to find the following:

1. Complex relationships
2. People under pressure
3. High stakes
4. Lack of control

As we explore these topics, be sure to try the brain-storming exercises that accompany them.

1. Complex Relationships

While human relationships are always complex, relationships in the workplace tend to be interdependent, competitive, hierarchical, public, and compulsory.

First, you rarely choose all the people in your organization, division, team, or workspace. Indeed, through selection processes, assignment decisions, and cubicle allocations, you're generally thrust into spending inordinate amounts of time with people who otherwise would be perfect strangers.

Second, you must do much more than coexist with your coworkers. You must depend upon them and they must depend upon you, routinely, even if they're the most significant competitors you face in your career.

Third, almost everyone you deal with at work is ranked in the organization chart; so you must grapple with explicit authority issues *and* implicit power dynamics.

BRAINSTORMING EXERCISE 1A

Directions: Consider the following questions.

1. *What impact does the compulsory nature of work relationships have on workplace anger? Does it cause anger? Does it exacerbate the effects of anger? Does it make it easier or harder to work through angry feelings?*

2. *What impact does overexposure to individuals at work have on workplace anger? Does it cause anger? Does it exacerbate the effects of anger? Does it make it easier or harder to work through angry feelings?*

➤

BRAINSTORMING EXERCISE CONT.　　　1A

3. *What impact does the interdependence of work relationships have on workplace anger? Does it cause anger? Does it exacerbate the effects of anger? Does it make it easier or harder to work through angry feelings?*

4. *What impact does the hierarchical nature of work relation- ships have on workplace anger? Does it cause anger? Does it exacerbate the effects of anger? Does it make it easier or harder to work through angry feelings?*

➤

BRAINSTORMING EXERCISE CONT.   1A

5. *What impact does the competitive nature of work relation-ships have on workplace anger? Does it cause anger? Does it exacerbate the effects of anger? Does it make it easier or harder to work through angry feelings?*

NOTES:

• *Exercise Concluded*

BRAINSTORMING EXERCISE   1B

Directions: Consider the following questions.

1. *With whom are you most likely to feel angry at work?*

   Subordinates?

   Peers?

   Your boss?

   Your entire team?

   The organization?

   The system?

   Vendors?

   Customers?

   Industry competitors?

2. *What kind of issues are most likely to prompt your anger with each of the following at work? And when?*

	WHAT ISSUES?	WHEN?
Subordinates		
Peers		
Your boss		
Your entire team		

   ➤

BRAINSTORMING EXERCISE CONT.	1B

	WHAT ISSUES?	WHEN?
The organization		
The system		
Vendors		
Customers		
Industry competitors		

3. *How do you generally resolve your anger with each of the following?*

Subordinates
Peers
Your boss
Your entire team
The organization
The system
Vendors
Customers
Industry competitors

➤

BRAINSTORMING EXERCISE CONT.	**I B**

4. *Who is most likely to feel angry with YOU at work?*

Subordinates?
Peers?
Your boss?
Your entire team?
The organization?
The system?
Vendors?
Customers?
Industry competitors?

5. *What kind of issues are most likely to prompt people's anger with YOU at work? And when?*

	WHAT ISSUES?	**WHEN?**
Subordinates		
Peers		
Your boss		
Your entire team		
The organization		
		➤

BRAINSTORMING EXERCISE CONT.		1B
	WHAT ISSUES?	**WHEN?**
The system		
Vendors		
Customers		
Industry competitors		

6. *How do people at work generally resolve their anger with YOU?*

Subordinates

Peers

Your boss

Your entire team

The organization

The system

Vendors

Customers

Industry competitors

• *Exercise Concluded*

2. People Under Pressure

Pressure in human relationships can come from many different sources, but most often it comes from a divergence in the best interests of the parties to the relationship. That divergence might be real or perceived; it might have to do with ends or means or both. The interests at stake might relate to expectations, needs, desires, or all of the above.

Even under the best of circumstances, it's difficult to keep the interests of two or more people in alignment for any extended period of time. Take a simple example: You and your spouse have a great relationship. You're driving down the highway together. She's late for an important business meeting, but you must use a lavatory ASAP. The divergence of your interests is likely to put more pressure on your relationship, at least temporarily.

Now think about this phenomenon in the workplace. Keeping the interests of you, your boss, your peers, your subordinates, your vendors, and your customers in alignment all the time is impossible. Meanwhile, you must also contend with competitors in your industry and their allies, whose interests are in direct opposition to yours.

Thus, for most people, work involves a constant juggling of, and wrestling with, competing interests. Whose interests are you going to attend to first? Whose interests might have to be sacrificed? Whose interests will be purposefully undermined? And how will you do this while protecting and advancing your own interests? That's where a lot of the pressure comes from.

BRAINSTORMING EXERCISE 1C

Directions: Consider the following questions.

1. *List some examples of competing interests in the workplace. How do your interests clash with the interests of others?*

Subordinates?

Peers?

Your boss?

Your entire team?

The organization?

The system?

Vendors?

Customers?

Industry competitors?

➤

1C

BRAINSTORMING EXERCISE CONT.

2. *How do their interests clash with the interests of each other?*

	Subor-dinates	Peers	Your boss	Your team	The organization	The system	Vendors	Custom-ers	Industry competitors
Subor-dinates									
Peers									
Your boss									
Your team									

BRAINSTORMING EXERCISE CONT.	Subordinates	Peers	Your boss	Your team	The organization	The system	Vendors	Customers	Industry competitors
									IC
The organization									
The system									
Vendors									
Customers									
Industry competitors									

BRAINSTORMING EXERCISE CONT. | IC

3. *How do you think the pressure of competing interests contributes to anger in the workplace? Does it cause anger? Does it exacerbate the effects of anger? Does it make it easier or harder to work through angry feelings?*

• *Exercise Concluded*

3. High Stakes

The stakes at work are always high—for you and for every person with whom you must deal. Why is that? For most people, work is the key to earning a living. As one fierce salesperson said to a competitor, "I don't hate you, but you're trying to take food off my family's table. So I will crush you if I can." Enough said.

Some people are focused on achieving a degree of financial security for the long term—they want to be free of the anxiety of living from paycheck to paycheck. For others, it may not be the money in the bank account that makes them feel secure, but rather, knowing that through their skills and hard work they can always earn money when necessary.

In the rare cases when earning a living and achieving some level of security is not a working person's primary career agenda, the stakes may be even higher. Work may be your primary creative outlet or your only creative outlet. Maybe work is your main source of self-esteem, the thing in your life that makes you feel smart, accomplished, respected, and important. Work might feel like your sphere of control and influence—your "turf." It could even be that you have a deep emotional connection to your work—that your work is your passion.

Remember this: You have a lot at stake and so does everyone else. Whether the stakes are financial or psychological or both, they are always on the line in every interaction at work. These stakes are on the line every time you pursue a goal, face a crisis, or see an opportunity. Not only is there pressure from competing interests, but the competition at work really matters to everyone involved.

BRAINSTORMING EXERCISE | 1D

Directions: Consider the following questions.

1. *What is at stake FOR YOU at work?*

   - Are the stakes financial or psychological, or both?
   - Do you have to work to put food on the table? If so, does that cause you anxiety?
   - Are you seeking financial security through your work?
   - Are you confident of your ability, in general, to earn money when necessary?
   - Is work your primary creative outlet?
   - Is work an important component of your self-esteem?
   - Do you feel like you have turf to protect in the workplace? If so, is that turf an area of responsibility, a team, or a physical work area?
   - Is your work your passion?

➤

BRAINSTORMING EXERCISE CONT.   ID

2. *Think about the stakes FOR YOU.*

   - What is the impact of having these stakes on the line at work?
   - What happens when you feel that your interests are threatened in some way?
   - How does having these stakes on the line affect your temper? Does it cause anger? Does it exacerbate the effects of anger? Does it make it easier or harder to work through angry feelings?

➤

BRAINSTORMING EXERCISE CONT.   1D

3. *Now think about some of the people with whom you deal at work. List one or more specific individuals in each of the following categories. Once you've done that, consider what might be at stake at work for each individual on the list. What is at stake for this person?*

Subordinates:

Peers:

Your boss:

Vendors:

Customers:

Industry competitors:

➤

BRAINSTORMING EXERCISE CONT.   ID

4. *Think about what might be at stake for any of the people listed above. Choose one person at a time and consider the following questions. (Note: You might choose someone with whom you clash in anger.)*

   - What do you think is the impact for this person of having these stakes on the line?
   - What do you think happens when this person feels that his or her interests are threatened in some way?
   - How does having these stakes on the line affect this person's temper? Does it cause anger? Does it exacerbate the effects of anger? Does it make it easier or harder to work through angry feelings?

• *Exercise Concluded*

4. Lack of Control

In the workplace, your circumstances and the circumstances of others can shift suddenly due to a wide range of factors beyond your control. There are so many variables, including:

— Geopolitical conditions

— National and local politics

— Weather and natural disasters

— Global economic shifts

— Changes in your industry, ranging from new competitors to new inventions

— Changes in your organization, ranging from mergers to new leadership to a new person on your team

The list goes on and on.

No matter how well you plan ahead, the unexpected is always lurking. You just don't know what it might be, when it might happen, and how much it might affect you and your plans. Now add this capricious element to a high-stakes workplace environment where you are already managing complex relationships with a whole bunch of individuals, many of whom have conflicting interests. It's no wonder that so many people feel a great deal of diffuse anxiety about their working lives and careers.

BRAINSTORMING EXERCISE   1E

Directions: Consider the following questions.

1. *List some of the factors that are totally out of your control that could have a huge impact on your circumstances at work.*

2. *Look over that list. Which factors make you feel most vulnerable? Are you aware of any feelings of anxiety about these factors? If so, does this anxiety affect your temper at work? Does it cause anger? Does it exacerbate the effects of anger? Does it make it easier or harder to work through angry feelings?*

➤

BRAINSTORMING EXERCISE CONT.　　　IE

3. *Look back on the last several months. Can you think of an unexpected factor out of your control that came up suddenly and made you feel threatened in some way? If so, what was the unexpected factor?*

- Was your fear warranted? Did this unexpected factor cause you any harm? If so, how did you react?
- Has it gone away, or is it still a threat? Is it still harming you? How are you reacting to it?
- Has this affected your relationship with anyone at work? If so, in what way?

➤

BRAINSTORMING EXERCISE CONT.   1E

4. *Again, look back on the last several months. Can you think of an unexpected factor out of your control that came up suddenly and made SOMEONE YOU MUST DEAL WITH REGULARLY feel threatened in some way? If so, what was the unexpected factor?*

   - Was the person's fear warranted? Did this unexpected factor cause him or her any harm? If so, how did he or she react?
   - Has it gone away, or is it still a threat? Is it still harming this person? How is he or she reacting to it?
   - Has this affected the person's relationship with you at work? If so, in what way?

• *Exercise Concluded*

Facing the Challenge of Anger in the Workplace

As much as individuals may struggle with anger in their personal lives, anger is even more challenging when it is felt and expressed in the workplace. Yes, anger is a normal, fundamental, and even healthy emotion rooted in our instinct for self-preservation. We need anger, just like we need fear. It gives us important data about our dealings with others, and it gives us the strength to face trouble and overcome obstacles. However, this powerful emotion can be dangerous as well. If it's not managed properly, anger can cause real harm to everyone involved. While the workplace environment is more likely to provoke feelings of anger, the consequences of poorly managed anger in the workplace may be much greater than in other contexts. At the same time, the potential benefits of anger in the workplace are also greater than in lower-stakes circumstances.

Managing anger effectively requires an understanding of both the costs and the potential benefits of anger. Once you recognize the necessity of managing anger, the key to success is learning to diagnose anger and then focusing on and addressing the *sources* of anger, rather than the emotion itself. You may have to deal with anger in you, in other individuals, in your team, and in your organization. The following chapters will give you the awareness, the best practices, and the concrete tools for tackling this challenge directly.

CHAPTER 2

The Costs of Anger in the Workplace

THE COSTS OF ANGER in the workplace can be devastating. Indeed, for many people the subject immediately evokes headlines of workplace shootings with terrible casualties. Such tragedies bear the highest price, from loss of life, serious injury, and psychological trauma to loss of productivity, property damage, and lingering confusion. They exemplify the most extreme, the most costly, and the most attention-getting manifestation of anger: actual violence. Fortunately, this is also the least common of anger's many forms. Most angry feelings never result in violence. However, they can still be very costly if poorly managed.

The costs of nonviolent anger in the workplace stem from cold, festering anger as well as angry outbursts; from anger that is expressed indirectly as well as directly; and even from anger that is never expressed at all. The harm caused by disruptive interactions, hurt feelings, and mental preoccupation with conflict and revenge may be obvious. But not so the more subtle costs of anger: personal damage ranging from diminished career prospects to diminished health; work-group damage ranging from lost work time to lost innovation; and organizational damage ranging from increased absenteeism to increased turnover. While it is difficult to calculate the monetary value of direct and indirect costs to individuals and organizations, we can enumerate some of the leading costly impacts of poorly managed anger.

Impact on the Angry Person

It was once thought that venting anger was healthier than holding it in. Today most findings indicate that angry people suffer negative effects whether they vent their feelings or not. Anger in the individual causes strong emotional and physical responses resulting in impaired cognitive and physical functioning. Poorly managed anger, then, can damage your career, and if the anger is chronic, it can result in long-term health problems.

Here are the specifics:

Immediate Emotional Components of Anger

- Increased impulsiveness
- Increased feeling of dominance
- Increased animation

- Diminished caution
- Diminished ability to reason

Immediate Physical Components of Anger

- Adrenal glands release.
- Epinephrine surges.
- Heart beats faster.
- Blood pressure rises.
- Muscles in chest, back, and arms may tense up.
- Body may sweat; flush or pale; feel clammy.

The Results of Anger:
Potential Career Problems

- Individuals carry secret or open grudges against you.
- You get a reputation for losing your temper.
- You get a reputation for abusing others.
- You become a target of lawsuits and non-juridical hearings.
- You become the target of illegal forms of revenge.
- You get a reputation for making judgment errors in the heat of the moment.
- Those with grudges against you try to thwart your explicit goals.

- People are less likely to want to work with you or for you.

- Risk-averse senior management tries to avoid having you on their projects.

- Clients, customers, and vendors try to avoid contact with you.

The Results of Anger: Long-Term Health Problems

- Weakened immune system

- Gastritis and other gastrointestinal tract illnesses

- Strokes

- Heart attacks

- Kidney disease

- Elevated blood pressure

- Headaches

- Respiratory disorders

- Skin disorders

- Arthritis

- Disabilities of the nervous system

- Circulatory disorders

In addition, anger can cause severe emotional problems and even result in suicide.

Impact on the Work Group and Organization

Anger's costs for the work group and organization go beyond the angry person. First, the target of the anger suffers considerable effects. Second, all those who are proximate to the angry relationship become susceptible to negative consequences. Third, the organization suffers not only from the diminished commitment and effort of the affected individuals, but also from the radiating impact of poorly managed anger.

People on the receiving end of anger generally experience emotional and physical effects similar to those experienced by the angry person. Additional emotional responses include fear, sadness, diminished self-esteem, preoccupation with the conflict, increased caution, and thoughts of revenge. In many cases, the targets of a more powerful person's anger eventually take out their retaliatory anger on someone entirely unrelated to the episode, usually someone less powerful. That's how anger from one superior can cascade down the ranks.

Another corollary effect occurs when the targets take out their retaliatory anger on peers and managers. However, when anger cascades upward, it is generally covert; for example, couched in a failure to cooperate, a failure to communicate, or an attempt to undermine the other person's goals.

According to one study (Pearson, Andersson, and Porath, 2000), the targets of anger most often respond with avoidance behavior that diminishes their work performance. These were the results for the subjects under study:

- Fifty-three percent lost work time worrying about the incident or future interactions.

- Thirty-seven percent believed that their commitment to the organization declined.

- Twenty-eight percent lost work time avoiding the instigator.

- Twenty-two percent put less effort into work.

- Ten percent spent less time at work.

- Twelve percent changed jobs to avoid the instigator.

As for others in the work group, they may suffer from their proximity to the angry relationship, feeling the lasting chill of its interactions. Those who are friendly with one or more of the principals in the relationship may be sought as allies. Others may simply be privy to what's going on and feel the collateral effects. Overall, individuals in the group may feel a diminished sense of trust in the principals or a general loss of safety in the group. This can result in a downward spiral of negative consequences.

The following is a summary of the dangers.

Consequences of Anger for the Work Group and Organization

- Increased relationship conflict (including jealousy, friction, and hostility)

- Lost work time

- Diminished
  - commitment
  - effort
  - information-sharing
  - risk-taking
  - collaboration
  - productivity
  - work quality
  - innovation

- Delayed decision-making

- Lack of good data for decision making

- Increased absenteeism and turnover

- Sabotage

- Litigation

- Verbal aggression

- Physical aggression

Perhaps the greatest damage to a work group or organization occurs when individuals perceive that egregious behavior from one person toward another has been tolerated and accepted by those in charge. When this happens, people feel let down by their leaders and begin to view the organization as unfair. They will often question the legitimacy of leaders who fail to take action. In cases where poorly managed anger is routinely tolerated and accepted by leadership, the organization may assume an angry culture, with negative effects flowing up the chain of command covertly and cascading down the chain of command all too obviously.

CHAPTER 3

The Benefits of Anger in the Workplace

MOST OF THE TIME, when we think of anger, we think of its negative effects, such as those covered in Chapter 2. That's why anger is often seen as *the forbidden emotion.* People who express anger are considered to be "irrational," and "out of control," two of the worst things that can be said about a person. This is particularly true in organizations, where people are supposed to leave their emotions at the workplace door. What many people don't realize—or never consider—is that anger in itself is neither positive nor negative. If managed effectively, anger can be a positive and productive emotion.

The Positive Side of Anger

As the exercise on the following pages illustrates, it's easier to determine the most productive response to anger when we're removed from the conflict and from angry feelings. At this distance, we can also better see anger's positive side.

➡ EXERCISE: Case Example

Directions: Read the case example below and then consider the questions that follow it.

Tim went into a performance-appraisal meeting expecting news of a healthy pay raise from his boss. He had been integral to a software-product team that had persevered through difficult circumstances to deliver a high-quality, highly marketable product. That the delivery had been several days over the promised deadline seemed negligible to Tim; the software already looked like it would be a major success.

However, at the meeting, his boss informed him that the company was being strict about deadlines. The team's late delivery thus meant he would not receive much of a raise. The boss was apologetic but stuck to the company guidelines, arguing that there were several points at which the team could have taken action to get the product out on time.

TIM WAS FURIOUS. He had worked many long days and nights to ensure the product would be a success. Now that devotion and hard work was to be overlooked in deference to a bureaucratic deadline? It was intolerable!

Questions for reflection

1. Is Tim's anger justified? Does his boss have a legitimate position, or is the boss being totally unreasonable? If Tim's anger is justified, who or what is the most appropriate target of his anger?

➤

EXERCISE: Case Example Cont.

2. What are some of the possible ways Tim could react to his anger?

3. How should Tim react to his anger?

4. Tim could do what he feels like doing: blow up at his boss, yell about how unfairly he's being treated, and storm out of the office threatening to quit.

   How would this reaction play out? What would be the impact on Tim? On the boss? On the work group? On the organization?

➤

EXERCISE: Case Example Cont.

5. Tim could do what he doesn't feel like doing: swallow his anger, express mild irritation to his boss, and return to his office determined to work far less hard next time—in fact, to limit his efforts to doing exactly what his boss wants, when his boss wants it, no more and no less.

   How would this reaction play out? What would be the impact on Tim? On the boss? On the work group? On the organization?

6. Tim could express his anger to his boss and use the anger's ENERGY in several ways:

   • To explain in detail how his team had exceeded the call of duty to get a high-quality product delivered close to deadline

   • To voice his disapproval of the deadline's strict enforcement as a policy that could promote diminished quality and lead to extended delays once deadlines have been missed

   ➤

EXERCISE: Case Example Cont.

- To ask his boss
  — to clarify the deadline policy,
  — to explain what the team should do next time to adjust a deadline if working as fast as possible and unable to meet the deadline,
  — to explain what methods the team should use to set more realistic deadlines in the future.

In addition, Tim could anticipate the next project and make a private commitment to lead by setting realistic deadlines, keeping close track of benchmarks on the way to deadline, and helping the team work smarter and faster to stay on course.

How would this reaction play out? What would be the impact on Tim? On the boss? On the work group? On the organization?

• *Exercise Concluded*

By considering a common anger scenario and imagining a productive response, we can see that conflicts in a dynamic group are not only necessary but also potentially productive.

Work groups must make decisions about the allocation of resources, the relative priority of goals, and the various means for reaching goals. Conflict, and the anger produced by conflict, shows that group members care about their product and are contributing diverse opinions. The twofold step of considering differences and resolving them is critical to any organization's efforts to adapt in a rapidly changing environment. That's why the leading research indicates that conflict over tasks within a work group contributes to better outcomes, even when the conflict is intense enough to provoke angry feelings, as long as people stay focused on the work itself—the resources allocated, goal setting, task planning, and execution.

When anger is focused **on the work itself**, it can become highly valuable. Such anger can do a number of things:

- Act as channel for energy that fuels intensive work and long hours

- Lead a person to persist against the odds in pursuit of difficult goals

- Act as a channel into creativity and innovation

- Prompt debate over competing points of view, resulting in better decisions

- Lead to the kind of healthy competition that drives productivity and quality

- Provide important data on policies, practices, relationships, behavior, and conditions

- Lead to improvements in the above when the data is handled properly

Of course, anger doesn't always remain focused on the work, even if it originated there. Often work-related anger degenerates into interpersonal anger. However, even interpersonal anger can be very valuable when managed effectively. It can do such positive things as:

- Lead to fruitful discussion, resolution, and action that dramatically improves a strained relationship

- Motivate a person to face strong competitors

- Motivate a person to confront wrongdoers

- Draw attention to injustice or perceived injustice

Complete the brainstorming exercise that concludes this chapter to see whether you have used work-focused anger in positive ways. If you find that you have not, then consider how you might use your anger more positively in the future.

BRAINSTORMING EXERCISE   3A

Directions: Consider the following questions.

1. *Have you ever had occasion to become angry about work itself—the resources allocated, goal setting, task planning, and/or task execution? If so, do you recall the details? When was this? What was at stake? Why were you angry? What happened as a result of your anger?*

2. *Have you ever used the energy of anger to fuel intensive work and long hours? If so, how did you do that?*

➤

BRAINSTORMING EXERCISE CONT. | 3A

3. *Has your anger ever lead you to persist against the odds in the pursuit of difficult goals? If so, how did it do that?*

4. *Have you ever channeled your anger into creativity and innovation? If so, how did you do that?*

5. *Has your anger ever led you to engage in a debate over competing points of view, resulting in better decisions? If so, how did it do that?*

➤

BRAINSTORMING EXERCISE CONT. 3A

6. *Has your anger ever lead you into healthy competition? If so, with whom? How did it play out?*

7. *Has your anger ever motivated you to face a strong competitor? If so, how did it motivate you?*

8. *Has your anger ever motivated you to confront wrongdoers? If so, how did it motivate you? How did the situation turn out?*

►

BRAINSTORMING EXERCISE CONT. | 3A

9. *Has your anger ever helped you draw attention to injustice? If so, how did your anger help you? How did the situation turn out?*

10. *Has your anger ever pointed to important data about policies, practices, relationships, behavior, and conditions? If so, what happened in response to that data? Did it lead to improvements? How do you feel about it now?*

➤

BRAINSTORMING EXERCISE CONT. | **3A**

11. *Have you ever had an experience where work-focused anger degenerated into interpersonal anger? If so, why did it do that? Did the anger lead to fruitful discussion, resolution, and action? Did it lead to improving a strained relationship? Why or why not?*

12. *Think of a time when expressing your anger had negative consequences. What happened? Now think of a time when expressing your anger had positive consequences. What happened? What do you think were the key differences between the two instances? Were there differences in the cause of the anger? In the people involved? In the way you handled the situation?*

• *Exercise Concluded*

CHAPTER 4

Diagnosing Anger

HOW DO YOU KNOW if anger is an issue in your workplace? Is there a way to find out if it is a cause of problems in you, another individual, your team, or your organization? Fortunately, because anger has distinct indications, it lends itself to diagnosis: the technique of identifying a condition from its signs and symptoms. To some extent, we're all familiar with medical diagnosis and its role in identifying diseases and other ailments. Those who are highly familiar with it, such as doctors and medical technicians, will tell you that diagnosis is as much an art as it is a science. Mastering any art requires practice, and to practice, you need guidelines. In the case of anger, what signs and symptoms should you be looking for?

Like medical diagnosis, anger diagnosis is complicated because its signs and symptoms vary considerably. Depending upon the gravity of the anger, the context in which the anger occurs, and the idiosyncrasies of each "patient," anger may be repressed or expressed; and if it is expressed, it may be expressed directly or indirectly.

The Over- and Under-Expression of Anger

Again, in thinking about anger and the problems that it causes in the workplace, we tend to focus on people who over-express their anger by behaving aggressively. However, as mentioned earlier, people who under-express anger pose an equally important problem. In some cases, such people are not even aware of their anger. In other cases, they feel anger but express it in subtle ways. Perhaps they don't want to seem out of control or they've been taught that shows of anger are bad and can only make a situation worse. Perhaps they work someplace where anger is tacitly forbidden, where people who express anger are shut down by others, especially in a work-group situation. Or maybe they're what psychologists refer to as "anger-in" types.

Researchers have long made a distinction between anger-out types and anger-in types. Anger-out types tend to experience intensely angry feelings and over-express those feelings in hostile behavior, such as door slamming, yelling, and throwing things. Anger-in types tend to under-express their anger. They suppress their feelings of anger and direct those feelings inward, harboring secret grudges.

As we learned in Chapter 2, it was once thought that venting anger, as anger-out types do, was healthier than repressing it, as anger-in types do. The release of anger supposedly relieved the stress of anger. Today, though, research findings indicate that intense feelings of anger, whether expressed outwardly *or* held in, can have serious long-term health effects on the individual. However, anger-out types are less apt to suffer the short-term health effects of repressed anger.

The repressed feelings of anger-in types may manifest themselves in headaches, stomach pain, skin disorders, breathing difficulties, back pain, and depression. It is critical to note, though, that people often suffer from these symptoms for reasons entirely unrelated to anger, so they alone do not afford a sufficient base for a diagnosis of anger. (In general, it's not a good idea for laypersons to attempt to connect physical illness to emotional sources.)

Of course, anger-out types display far more symptoms as they're more likely to behave in obviously aggressive ways when angry. Aggression is an action response intended to inflict pain or discomfort on others. Its various forms are outlined in the next section.

When Anger Becomes Aggression

The most dreaded impacts of anger are those that come from aggression. Aggression can be physical or verbal;

active or passive; direct or indirect. The matrix below organizes the various forms of workplace aggression within these categories.

MATRIX: WORKPLACE AGGRESSION		
TYPE	Direct	Indirect
Physical: Active	Homicide Assault Sexual assault Dirty looks Obscene gestures	Theft Sabotage Defacing property Consuming needed resources

Physical: Passive	Intentional work
	  slowdowns
	Refusing to provide
	  needed resources
	Leaving area when
	  target enters
		Showing up late for
		  meetings
		Delaying work to make
		  target look bad
		Failing to protect the
		  target's welfare

Verbal: Active	Threats
	Yelling
	Insults and sarcasm
	Flaunting status
	Unfair performance
	  evaluation
		Spreading rumors
		Whistle-blowing
		Belittling opinions
		Attacking protégé
		Transmitting damaging
		  information

Verbal: Passive	Failing to return phone
	  calls
	Giving target the silent
	  treatment
	Refusing target's request
	Damning with faint
	  praise
		Failing to transmit
		  information
		Failing to deny false
		  rumors
		Failing to warn of
		  impending dangers
		Failing to defend target

CHART DRAWN FROM A STUDY BY NEUMAN AND BARON, 1997

When you identify such acts of aggression, it is safe to say that you have diagnosed an expression of anger. Active and direct forms of aggression are the easiest signs and symptoms to identify, while passive and indirect forms are the most difficult. It is a mixed blessing that passive and indirect forms are by far the most common. They are less noticeable and less damaging in the short term, but for these reasons they can continue without remedy for significant periods of time. This can result in considerable damage to interpersonal relationships and team performance as well as the organization as a whole.

Be aware of anger's more subtle and insidious signs and symptoms so you can deal with them before they turn into the more dangerous acts of direct and active aggression.

Three Common Syndromes

You should also be aware of three syndromes that commonly occur in organizations:

1. Cascading anger
2. The angry star
3. The culture of undue politeness

I. Cascading Anger

The over-expression of anger can have significant negative effects when directed downward from superiors to subordinates. Higher-powered individuals who, under little threat of retaliation, use their positions in this way set off a cascade of negative anger expression throughout the organization. Once it's perceived as acceptable for CEOs to yell at their secretaries, then senior vice-presidents begin yelling at their subordinates, group vice-presidents begin yelling at their subordinates, and so on, down the line.

People who are on the receiving end of this anger, being unable to vent their anger at its true target, will release it in other ways, usually by venting at someone less powerful than they are. They also may release it by lowering their commitment to the organization or by engaging in low-level sabotage or pilfering. Sometimes they repress the anger until they get home, where it becomes directed at their spouse and kids. Unchecked, this cascading anger from the top of the organizational hierarchy can have severe consequences for the whole organization.

2. The Angry Star

In this syndrome, the organization allows certain high-performing individuals to direct anger in unchecked ways at those around them. Such "favoritism" is more apt to develop in companies where each employee's financial performance is measurable, as in investment banks and law firms. Managers may tolerate individuals who generate high revenues for the firm but make life miserable for coworkers and subordinates—those on the receiving end of anger.

This is a particularly difficult pattern to break, as the goal of bottom-line profits suggests retaining these individuals at all cost, despite their negative effects on others. There is a problem with this limited view of profit, though: It rarely takes into account the possible long-term hits to profit brought about by unchecked anger.

3. The Culture of Undue Politeness

On the opposite end of the spectrum are organizations that do not tolerate any expressions of anger, or any negative emotions at all, in the professed desire to encourage civility and politeness. Although these organizations may gain cohesiveness from pleasant interchanges and interpersonal respect, they are likely to lose vital information in the process. By forcing people to repress anger, they also may prompt indirect and passive expressions of anger, set off health problems, and cause diminished commitment and performance. Moreover, they lose the benefits of effectively managed anger. Of course, civility should always be encouraged in the workplace; but people must also be allowed to express anger in safe and productive ways.

For help with diagnosing anger, see the signs and symptoms inventory on the next page. Also, try out the brainstorming exercise that follows it.

DIAGNOSING ANGER:
SIGNS AND SYMPTOMS INVENTORY

Are any of the following signs or symptoms present in your organization, your team, or anyone you know in your workplace?

- Homicide:
- Assault:
- Sexual assault:
- Dirty looks:
- Obscene gestures:

- Intentional work slowdowns:
- Refusing to provide needed resources:
- Leaving area when someone enters:

- Threats:
- Yelling:
- Insults and screams:
- Flaunting status:
- Unfair performance evaluation:

- Failing to return phone calls:
- Giving someone the silent treatment:
- Refusing someone's request:
- Damning with faint praise:

- Theft:
- Sabotage:
- Defacing property:
- Consuming needed resources:

- Showing up late for meetings:
- Delaying work to make someone look bad:
- Failing to protect someone's welfare:　➤

SIGNS AND SYMPTOMS INVENTORY CONT.

- Spreading rumors:
- Whistle-blowing:
- Belittling opinions:
- Attacking protégé:
- Transmitting damaging information:

- Failing to transmit information:
- Failing to deny false rumors:
- Failing to warn of impending dangers:
- Failing to defend someone:

• *Inventory Concluded*

BRAINSTORMING EXERCISE　4A

Directions: Consider the following questions.

1. *Is over-expression of anger a problem for you? For anyone you know at work? For your team? For your organization? If so, how do you know it's a problem? What are the signs and symptoms?*

➤

BRAINSTORMING EXERCISE CONT. | **4A**

2. *Is under-expression of anger a problem for you? For anyone you know at work? For your team? For your organization? If so, how do you know it's a problem? What are the signs and symptoms?*

3. *Think about yourself for a moment. Are you an anger-in or anger-out type? How do you know? What are the signs and symptoms?*

➤

BRAINSTORMING EXERCISE CONT.   **4A**

4. *Think of someone at work who seems opposite in type from you. (If you are anger-in, think of an anger-out person. If you are anger-out, think of an anger-in person.) How do you know? What are the signs and symptoms?*

5. *Is the cascading anger syndrome a problem for you? For anyone you know at work? For your team? For your organization? If so, how do you know it's a problem? What are the signs and symptoms?*

➤

BRAINSTORMING EXERCISE CONT.   **4A**

6. *Is the angry star syndrome a problem for you? For anyone you know at work? For your team? For your organization? If so, how do you know it's a problem? What are the signs and symptoms?*

7. *Is the culture of undue politeness syndrome a problem for you? For anyone you know at work? For your team? For your organization? If so, how do you know it's a problem? What are the signs and symptoms?*

• *Exercise Concluded*

A Concluding Note

In concluding this chapter, we would like to note that anger can be such a serious emotional problem for some individuals that professional counseling or medical assistance is required. Our information here is not intended to take the place of professional diagnosis; rather, it is intended to equip you with anger's basic signs and symptoms so that you can recognize anger when you see it, even if it is disguised.

CHAPTER 5

Focus on the Source

WHENEVER YOU DIAGNOSE ANGER as an issue in your workplace, you must be ready to take action. This is true whether anger is an issue for you, another individual, your team, or your organization. The problem is, when we deal with anger, we tend to focus on the feelings of anger and their outward expressions. That's because they make us feel uncomfortable. Our goal thus becomes to "stop the yelling" and get people to "calm down." But, as necessary as that goal might be in some situations, it doesn't resolve the anger—it's like trying to put out a fire by chasing the smoke. Anger is an effect; for every instance of it, there is at least one cause.

An effective anger-management strategy goes far beyond the firefighting that temporarily maintains civility. The true key to resolving anger and tapping its benefits is to focus on the *source.* By identifying and addressing the underlying causes of anger, you can use the data provided by the anger to continually improve relationships as well as systems, practices, and policies.

The Causes of Anger in the Workplace

Each episode of anger has a unique source—a particular combination of causes. What are those causes in the workplace? In academic and journalistic studies of anger, researchers often ask people what makes them angry at work. Here is a list of their typical responses:

- The way my boss/supervisor treats me
- Stupid company policies
- Coworkers who don't do their fair share
- Not enough control over assignments
- Not enough pay
- Not enough benefits
- Tight deadlines
- Too much work
- Coworkers making careless mistakes
- Dealing with rude customers
- Lack of cooperation
- Stupidity and ignorance
- How the company treats coworkers
- How the company treats me

While people may differ in the specifics of what makes them angry, the causes usually have one common denominator: interpersonal dynamics—relationships between and among people. Every person has a basic need to value him- or herself and to feel valued by others. Yet when people's self-esteem is threatened, they're reluctant to admit it, even to themselves.

Some leading psychologists argue that anger is driven by primary emotions that attack self-esteem; these include feelings of betrayal, disapproval, deprivation, exploitation, frustration, humiliation, manipulation, restriction, and threat. Such emotions can be traced to any of a wide range of causes, from broad contextual circumstances to highly personal impulses. We may categorize the causes into five troublesome areas:

1. Anger at the system
2. Perceived inequity
3. Blocked goals
4. Divergent values
5. Unequal power relations

1. Anger at the System

Today many factors beyond our control create a broad context more likely to produce anger. In our highly interdependent and interconnected global economy, events halfway around the world can come knocking on our door and make us feel threatened and insecure.

Downsizing, increased workloads, and uncertainty about the fate of markets and organizations cause worry and anger—stress all around. People are spending more time at work—where they are expected to work harder, faster, smarter, and better—and working closely with one another in small groups and teams, thus creating more settings for emotions to be exhibited and shared. Performance standards have risen, but job security is a thing of the past. The increase of dual-career families has caused added pressure; couples often have to deal with frazzling commutes and nightmarish child-care logistics, and bring their increased anxiety to work.

In too many organizations, management accepts incivility, disrespect, and over-the-top anger. Employees are expected to take abuse as a hurdle to organizational success. Meanwhile, norms of civility and politeness in society as a whole continue to erode. Television offers a vision of immediate gratification, in which problems are easily solved by the show's end. Employees nurtured on these messages are not ready for the frustration of real life, where nothing may be solved by the day's end—or even the week's end.

Many of us work in organizations that are so large, so bureaucratized, and so departmentalized, we find it difficult to identify the cause of our anger. This may deepen our anger because it makes us feel out of control. Anger, by its very nature, is a feeling directed at a *proximate cause*—we want to aim anger at something or someone in particular. When large organizational systems with complex rules and procedures obscure our "target," we may grow angry at the system itself.

Systemic problems are by nature difficult to fix. But anger at the system is a signal that everything is *not* okay, at least not for everybody. It is important to be aware of this context when looking for more acute causal factors.

2. Perceived Inequity

As individuals, we have a strong tendency to compare ourselves to others. If we find that by some measure we are doing better than they are (perhaps we make more money or have a better job), we usually feel good; if we find that we are not doing as well, we usually feel bad. But this kind of personal difference is not the same thing as inequity. Inequity is a lack of fairness and justice. When we become aware of differences that seem unfair or unjust—especially when they have to do with issues we find important—we can experience strong feelings of resentment and anger.

In the workplace, we tend to look at what other people get (monetary reward, praise, and promotion) in relation to what they contribute (how hard they work, how smart they are). We also tend to work out in our heads what we get in relation to what we give. If it looks like another person is getting a better "deal" based on these equations, then we tend to get angry.

It is critical for managers to recognize employees' feelings of inequity. One of the most common reasons for employee violence and theft is not personal gain, but the desire to regain a sense of justice and fair play. For instance, after company mergers and acquisitions, employee theft tends to increase. Why? Because people feel that their job security is threatened. They're stressed about the organizational change and fearful about how they'll fit into the new regime. They feel they're likely to get lost in the shuffle and to suffer for reasons over which they have no control or even influence. In short, they engage in such behavior because they want to "balance the situation."

People who seek to "avenge" perceived wrongs done to them by the organization see themselves as having a moral cause; that's what makes the depth of anger (and the negative behaviors it can cause) seem so extreme. The cause may actually be a long-term set of perceived inequities and injustices that a person groups together.

When perceived inequity is driving anger, the first question we must ask is whether there is true inequity that must be resolved. Sometimes the perception of inequity stems from a lack of information. One might think: "Mary gets Thursdays off, and I don't. That's not fair." Just adding a piece of information can change the perception: "Mary works on Saturdays, and you don't. So she gets Thursdays off to make up for it." This is one reason why some transparency is preferable to secrecy in employer-employee dealings. Every deal is different and negotiated on its own terms with its own rationale. Such terms are less likely to be perceived as unfair if the rationale for the deal is transparent and expectations are clear.

3. Blocked Goals

All purposeful action involves the pursuit of goals. Our most basic human goals have to do with survival: protecting ourselves and our territory. But goals range in scope from great to small, whether the goal is mastering a technical skill or walking from your kitchen table to the living-room couch. We go about living by accomplishing one goal after another, from the most basic to the most extravagant. That's why most people become extremely frustrated when the pursuit of their goals is blocked in some way. The most common source of blocked goals is another person or group in pursuit of different goals.

In the workplace, goal-setting is at its most formal and the accomplishment of goals is explicitly and singularly valued. When two or more individuals or groups work together but have different goals, sometimes those goals come into conflict. In some cases, there is a clash in overall objectives, though usually the overall objectives are the same for everyone—profit. Problems more typically develop from a difference in shorter-term imperatives. For example, a sales group promises more than a service group can deliver, meaning that customers are always making inordinate demands, causing overwork and stress; the service group disappoints customers and interferes with subsequent sales efforts.

Similar goal clashes also may occur between and among individuals. Perhaps a manager's goal is to increase productivity, but his subordinate's goal is to slow down and enjoy the work. Or maybe a team member's goal is to get all the work done quickly and go home early, while her teammate's goal is to take a long time to complete a project so the team can collect overtime pay.

Of course, it is not the case that differing goals must always clash. Communication about alternative methods or even alternative goals can lead to healthy coexistence and even synergy. This requires trust and a likelihood of benefit to both parties.

When differing goals are mutually exclusive, decisions must be made. Which goal is more important? What adjustments can be made to the goals that are secondary to the more important goal?

Keep in mind that sometimes goals are blocked by circumstances that have nothing to do with competing goals. Even a factor as neutral as the weather can present an obstacle. The blockage is no less frustrating, though, and causes no less anger. By thinking creatively about what is causing the goal blockage, you may be able to circumvent the angry response. By removing the barriers—if doing so is realistic and appropriate—you can often turn a potentially negative situation into a positive one. If you cannot remove the barriers, then you must be prepared to deal with the frustration and anger that the blocked goals are likely to cause.

4. Divergent Values

When others behave in ways that we find abhorrent, we usually become angry—such behavior seems an affront to our values. In general, people vary in what they regard as abhorrent. But in the workplace, most people value competence, hard work, and integrity, and so are likely to get angry when they perceive a disregard or violation of these values.

Incompetence or laziness in a coworker, subordinate, or superior offends our sense of efficiency and hinders work-group productivity. It also may have long-term effects with respect to damaged client relationships or high monetary cost. Behavior that is considered morally reprehensible—such as stealing, cheating, taking advantage of others, and harassing people—is particularly noxious because it may involve direct damage to others.

It is important to understand that this type of anger is based on blame and the perception of intent. The angry person *blames* the offender for a misdeed of some type because he or she thinks the offender *intended* to cause harm. Managers must be prepared to consider intent without playing judge and jury.

No matter how infuriating incompetence may be, nobody intends to be incompetent. When a person acts incompetent in order to evade responsibility, the problem is a combination of laziness and dishonesty. Incompetence per se results from failures in selection, training, and/or supervision; thus when we are faced with true incompetence, the appropriate target of anger is management, not the incompetent worker.

In the case of laziness and failure of integrity, the appropriate target of anger is equally clear. The reaction should be swift and the offender evaluated. Does the offender *understand* that he or she has engaged in behavior that is unacceptable in the workplace? Does this person understand that the behavior will not be tolerated? Will he or she be given another chance?

In terms of assigning blame, we also need to remember an important finding from psychological research: that people have a tendency to blame people rather than circumstances when a problem crops up. For example, if a team is about to give a major presentation and a member has lost data vital to that presentation, most people will blame the member, at least initially, rather than factors beyond the member's control. Their first thought is that the member is incompetent, lazy, or dishonest, not that something like a computer glitch or a virus is the actual culprit. Why do people do this? Because it's easier to be angry at a person than at a situation.

Considering this natural tendency to look for blame-worthy intent, we must be careful to check the facts when we believe a person is at fault or intended negative consequences. Good people make unintentional mistakes, and good people are the victims of factors beyond their control.

5. Unequal Power Relations

Organizations are structured on hierarchical relation-ships, and such relationships, by their very nature, generate fear and anger—the less powerful fearing the more powerful, with anger flowing in both directions. Typically, the less powerful figure is angry that the more powerful figure holds the key to his or her fear. And the more powerful figure is angered whenever that power is questioned or threatened because it confers a feel-ing of control and security in the relationship.

Anger may flow both ways, but it is more apt to be ex-pressed in the downward flow. For example, according to one study, in situations where employees were an-gry with their bosses, only 45 percent expressed their feelings immediately, during the anger-eliciting event; however, 58 percent expressed their anger immediately toward coworkers, and 71 percent when anger was directed at subordinates.

Why does anger's expression tend to flow downward in organizations? First, those with hierarchical power feel the need to display and test their power periodically. Second, they become accustomed to the fruits of their power and insensitive to its impact on subordinates.

For subordinates, of course, that power and its impact are considerable. Just think. The more powerful make demands on their subordinates' time, impose goals and deadlines, evaluate competence and performance, and determine people's chances of promotion and success. Unfortunately, too often they also treat subordinates with disrespect, freely castigating them or otherwise lowering their self-esteem.

In any relationship, disrespect—treating others in a way that denies their fundamental worth—is likely to cause anger. When directed at someone who already feels powerless or dependent, it creates potent feelings of anger and a sense of unfairness. That's why studies show that people who are angry with their bosses link the offense to unfairness—an issue not as significant when anger is directed at coworkers or subordinates.

Because those in authority represent the "system" and have far-ranging responsibilities—from making decisions about burdens and rewards to enforcing standards of performance and conduct—they are not only the most likely to express anger in the workplace, but also the most likely to provoke anger in subordinates.

➥ EXERCISE: Case Examples

FOCUSING ON THE SOURCE OF ANGER

Directions: Consider each case example below and evaluate the source of the anger.

CASE EXAMPLE A

"I've had two or three instances of absolute loss of control, when I was just so mad that I could've kicked a hole in the wall. Actually, I did do that once. A blood bank that left us without blood for a critically ill patient sent me into a raging, screaming fit. The blood wasn't for one of my patients. I just happened to be near the recovery room when a big mess developed with a patient. The patient was rapidly losing blood, and we should've had blood an hour earlier but didn't.

"I'd had it up to here with the blood bank not coming through on promises, not getting us blood when we needed it—this had been a frustrating problem for years and years. Finally, I lost my temper. I demanded the administrator get up there or some other person in charge. I had operating-room supervisors there.

"Later I learned that the hospital had instituted a new computerized process for ordering blood, and that there were certain steps you had to follow to get it."

1. What is the source of the anger in this case example? Who is angry? At whom? And why?

➤

EXERCISE: Case Examples Cont.

2. Is the person angry at the system? Angry because of some perceived inequity? Because of blocked goals? Because of divergent values? Because of unequal power?

3. Is the angry person's self-esteem being threatened in some way? If so, how?

4. Does the angry person feel betrayed? Disapproved of? Deprived? Exploited? Frustrated? Humiliated? Manipulated? Restricted? Threatened?

5. Focusing on the true source of the anger in this case, what data is the anger providing? What action can be taken in response to that data?

➤

EXERCISE: Case Examples Cont.

CASE EXAMPLE B

"We were trying to figure out the schedule, and there was a lot of tension. People want certain hours and get really stressed when they can't have them.

"This one particular time I asked for hours on Saturday and a coworker said, 'Why can't you take a Sunday?' I thought it was kind of odd that she was even asking. Was it really any of her business? I told her that I had something I needed to do on Sunday. And she replied, 'Well, you know how I feel about that.' Meaning that she didn't think it was fair that people who go to church on Sunday should always get Saturday hours. I said to her, 'That's your opinion,' and she snapped at me. And I snapped right back."

1. What is the source of the anger in this case example? Who is angry? At whom? And why?

2. Is the person angry at the system? Angry because of some perceived inequity? Because of blocked goals? Because of divergent values? Because of unequal power?

➤

EXERCISE: Case Examples Cont.

3. Is the angry person's self-esteem being threatened in some way? If so, how?

4. Does the angry person feel betrayed? Disapproved of? Deprived? Exploited? Frustrated? Humiliated? Manipulated? Restricted? Threatened?

5. Focusing on the true source of the anger in this case, what data is the anger providing? What action can be taken in response to that data?

➤

EXERCISE: Case Examples Cont.

CASE EXAMPLE C

"We draw for holiday time off, for getting two weeks off at Christmas. We drew for the next five years. I won't get a Christmas vacation for a few years. My son decided to get married during the holidays, so I asked the person who had drawn for it this time if she would be willing to either modify her vacation time or trade with me or something. She already had plans, she said, so that was frustrating for me.

"We have such a small pool, there's just not a lot of flexibility. So when you have life events like that, it's really frustrating not to have the freedom to manipulate, to some degree, your personal leave."

1. What is the source of the anger in this case example? Who is angry? At whom? And why?

2. Is the person angry at the system? Angry because of some perceived inequity? Because of blocked goals? Because of divergent values? Because of unequal power?

▶

EXERCISE: Case Examples Cont.

3. Is the angry person's self-esteem being threatened in some way? If so, how?

4. Does the angry person feel betrayed? Disapproved of? Deprived? Exploited? Frustrated? Humiliated? Manipulated? Restricted? Threatened?

5. Focusing on the true source of the anger in this case, what data is the anger providing? What action can be taken in response to that data?

▶

EXERCISE: Case Examples Cont.

CASE EXAMPLE D

"We have a lot of frustration right now with our supervisor. The real problem is a feeling of not being included, not knowing exactly where we stand or what our supervisor expects from the staff. We're becoming frustrated because he'll expect us to do something, and when we don't do it because we didn't know we were supposed to, we get in trouble.

The supervisor's approach is belittling to us. We don't feel like we are listened to, and it doesn't matter what we say or what we don't."

1. What is the source of the anger in this case example? Who is angry? At whom? And why?

2. Is the person angry at the system? Angry because of some perceived inequity? Because of blocked goals? Because of divergent values? Because of unequal power?

➤

EXERCISE: Case Examples Cont.

3. Is the angry person's self-esteem being threatened in some way? If so, how?

4. Does the angry person feel betrayed? Disapproved of? Deprived? Exploited? Frustrated? Humiliated? Manipulated? Restricted? Threatened?

5. Focusing on the true source of the anger in this case, what data is the anger providing? What action can be taken in response to that data?

➤

EXERCISE: Case Examples Cont.

CASE EXAMPLE E

"A lot of times people don't pick up [after themselves, and so] you have extra [work to do] at the end of the day. You're trying to hustle, and it feels like you don't get anywhere. It is those people who don't pull their share. They know what they are doing. You want other people that you are working with to have a good day. You try not to show [your anger], but it doesn't always work."

1. What is the source of the anger in this case example? Who is angry? At whom? And why?

2. Is the person angry at the system? Angry because of some perceived inequity? Because of blocked goals? Because of divergent values? Because of unequal power?

3. Is the angry person's self-esteem being threatened in some way? If so, how?

▶

EXERCISE: Case Examples Cont.

4. Does the angry person feel betrayed? Disapproved of? Deprived? Exploited? Frustrated? Humiliated? Manipulated? Restricted? Threatened?

5. Focusing on the true source of the anger in this case, what data is the anger providing? What action can be taken in response to that data?

CASE EXAMPLE F

"Joe is very aggressive and manipulative. He has thrown up barriers for me on almost a daily basis since I've taken this job. We even lost an employee over the way Joe treated her. We've had some pretty big communication problems with him, too. He's sarcastic, backbites a lot, and belittles his co-workers in front of [clients]. This has gone on for well over a year.

"So I called a meeting to set some ground rules for behavior in the department. During this meeting, Joe was obviously very angry and threw out an offensive comment that was

EXERCISE: Case Examples Cont.

clearly directed at me. I finally reached the point where I had to say, 'I do this because it is my job to do this. This is what I am responsible for, accountable for, so this is why I make these decisions.'

I could see that Joe was flushed and shaky. I couldn't tell whether he was going to cry or blow his stack. I think he felt really frustrated that things didn't go his way.

"I don't know about long-term effects. If nothing else I think he left the meeting with a much clearer perspective of what the expectations are in terms of treatment of other members of the group and what his role is versus my role."

1. What is the source of the anger in this case example? Who is angry? At whom? And why?

2. Is the person angry at the system? Because of some perceived inequity? Because of blocked goals? Because of divergent values? Because of unequal power?

▶

EXERCISE: Case Examples Cont.

3. Is the angry person's self-esteem being threatened in some way? If so, how?

4. Does the angry person feel betrayed? Disapproved of? Deprived? Exploited? Frustrated? Humiliated? Manipulated? Restricted? Threatened?

5. Focusing on the true source of the anger in this case, what data is the anger providing? What action can be taken in response to that data?

➤

EXERCISE: Case Examples Cont.

CASE EXAMPLE G

"As Director of Nursing, I was furious at a certain night nurse and had to fire her. A patient died, and he probably didn't have to. He had fallen two or three times during the night shift, and the documentation was not good. The nurse didn't take the oxygen-level stats, and we never got vital signs, which would have been a good indication of what was happening with the patient. Why did this man fall? You have to ask yourself lots of questions in such a situation, and even though we are limited here, there are many things the nurse could have done. She did not do CPR. She apparently did not know the patient was in full code. She did not have all the information that she should have had.

"I thought she had been on the wing long enough to have learned those kinds of things. Very few people here are full code, so you just know who is full code on your wing. I probably should have fired her long before this happened."

1. What is the source of the anger in this case example? Who is angry? At whom? And why?

2. Is the person angry at the system? Angry because of some perceived inequity? Because of blocked goals? Because of divergent values? Because of unequal power?

EXERCISE: Case Examples Cont.

3. Is the angry person's self-esteem being threatened in some way? If so, how?

4. Does the angry person feel betrayed? Disapproved of? Deprived? Exploited? Frustrated? Humiliated? Manipulated? Restricted? Threatened?

5. Focusing on the true source of the anger in this case, what data is the anger providing? What action can be taken in response to that data?

• *Exercise Concluded*

MANAGEMENT TOOL:
CLARIFYING THE SOURCE OF ANGER

Directions: Use this tool to evaluate incidents of anger and to search for their underlying causes.

THE FACTS

• Who is angry?

• At whom?

• Why?

CAUSAL FACTORS

• Is the angry person angry at the system?

• Angry because of some perceived inequity?

• Angry because of divergent values?

• Angry because of unequal power?

EVALUATE THE ANGRY PERSON'S FEELINGS

• Is the angry person's self-esteem being threatened in some way? If so, how?

➤

MANAGEMENT TOOL CONT.

- Does the angry person feel ...
  - Betrayed?
  - Disapproved of?
  - Deprived?
  - Exploited?
  - Frustrated?
  - Humiliated?
  - Manipulated?
  - Restricted?
  - Threatened?

CONSIDERING ACTION
- What data is the anger providing?

- What action can be taken in response to that data?
  - Goals:

  - Deadlines:

  - Guidelines:

  - Next steps:

• Tool Concluded

CHAPTER 6

Dealing With
Your Own Anger

WHILE WE ARE TYPICALLY QUITE AWARE of other people's anger tendencies, many of us have a blind spot when it comes to thinking about and dealing with our own anger. It is imperative to address this deficiency before focusing on the workplace. You cannot effectively manage anger in other individuals, your team, or your organization unless you can understand and deal with your own anger.

Remember that anger is a complex emotional response that involves both thinking (cognition) and feeling (physical effects). Anger can have many different causes and can be expressed in many different ways. Becoming more aware of your anger means exploring several issues:

- Do you have a tendency towards anger?

- What kinds of things make you angry?

- How angry do you generally become?

- How do you typically deal with your anger?

The following self-assessment will help you to think through these issues for yourself. It is intended for you alone. Be honest with yourself.

✦ SELF-ASSESSMENT:
Exploring Your Own Anger

---

1. Do you think that you are an angry person in general? Either way, what makes you think so?

2. Has anyone ever told you that you are an angry person or that you have issues with anger? If so, who? Under what circumstances? How many times have you heard that?

3. How often would you say that you get angry?

➤

SELF-ASSESSMENT CONT.

4. When you do get angry, how angry do you usually get? Mildly irritated? Irritated? Mad? Enraged?

5. How often would you say that you become enraged? What things tend to enrage you? Why do you think these things enrage you?

6. How often would you say that you become irritated? What things tend irritate you? Why do these things irritate you?

7. Do you sometimes become angry over small inconveniences or relatively inoffensive statements made by others? If so, how often does this sort of thing happen? Why do you think it happens?

➤

SELF-ASSESSMENT CONT.

8. How do you behave when you become angry? Would you say that you are an anger-in type or anger-out?

9. Do you sometimes harm others or damage property as a result of your anger? If so, how often does this sort of thing happen? Why do you think it happens?

10. Do you sometimes hide your anger and avoid telling others what is bothering you? If so, how often does this sort of thing happen? Why do you think it happens?

11. Do you sometimes withdraw and become uncommunicative when you are angry? If so, how often does this sort of thing happen? Why do you think it happens?

• Assessment Concluded

Anger is one of the most difficult emotions to explore, so congratulations on completing the self-assessment. Perhaps you're one small step closer now to understanding your own anger.

If you think that you have problems with chronic anger—if you have repeatedly harmed others directly or indirectly with your anger or if others have observed that you have a violent temper—you should consider the help of a psychotherapist. However, even with the assistance of a professional (or someone whom you trust deeply and who knows you well), ultimately it is you who must evaluate and address your anger. Many people go through their entire lives without ever examining their deep feelings rigorously and honestly. All of us need to do this, though.

Six-Step Process for Managing Your Anger

Once you've grappled with your feelings, the next challenge is managing your anger by following these steps:

1. Avoid anger.

2. Calm yourself physically.

3. Think logically.

4. Express your feelings appropriately and effectively.

5. Seek solutions to the underlying causes of your anger.

6. Let it go.

I. Avoid Anger

When thinking about this important step, keep in mind the wide range of things likely to cause anger; for example, big-picture (systemic) causes, blocked goals, perceived inequity, divergent values, and unequal power relationships.

If you lead an active life, have a busy career, and interact with many people, you cannot isolate yourself from every external irritant. You're going to sit in traffic jams, be put on hold when making business calls, and so on. Sometimes you will get less than your fair share, or your children will, or your parents will, or your friends will. You won't make every sale or meet every deadline. You will probably work with people who are less diligent than you, less competent than you, or less honest than you. You will probably have a boss, or a teacher, or a family member, or a customer who has power over you. And you will probably find yourself with power over others.

Even if you could hide from every environmental factor likely to anger you, you still would be vulnerable to internal causes of anger. You might be mad at yourself for placing such restrictions on your life, for depriving

yourself of all that the outside world has to offer. You
might feel that others disapprove of your hiding. And
so forth.

Although you cannot hide from the causes of anger, you
can take steps that make you less susceptible to them.
If you feel happy, confident, and in control, then you
are less likely to respond as strongly to anger stimuli.
Try these steps:

- *Consider your environment and lifestyle.*

- *Examine your outlook on life.*

- *Start taking better care of yourself.*

Consider Your Environment and Lifestyle

Start by compiling a list of the things that make you
angry; then see whether you can avoid any of them or
at least make helpful adjustments. The worksheet on
the next page will help you.

For another approach, take a look at your typical daily
schedule and then fill in the details. Be as thorough as
possible about what you usually do each hour:

— Where are you, with whom, doing what,
and how?

Then think about which aspects of your environment
and lifestyle are most likely to make you feel angry.

WORKSHEET:
WHAT MAKES YOU ANGRY?

Directions: Record a list of things that make you angry; then consider whether any of them can be avoided or if you can make helpful adjustments.

What Makes You Angry?	How to Avoid Factor or Adjust It

Can you think of adjustments that might reduce the anger? For example:

- If you and your spouse tend to fight at a certain time each day, perhaps you can make it a point to cross paths at a different time.

- If your commute drives you crazy, maybe there's an alternative mode of transportation you can use or an alternative time you can travel.

- If you hate your officemate, maybe you can move to a different workspace.

- If you become angry when you watch the evening news, maybe you can read the newspaper instead.

Record your details on the "Environmental and Lifestyle Inventory," which begins on the next page.

Examine Your Outlook on Life

How do you feel about the world around you? How do you feel about yourself? What possible adjustments would make you feel better about the world and yourself?

Clarify these matters by using the "Personal Inventory," which follows the "Environmental and Lifestyle Inventory."

ENVIRONMENTAL AND LIFESTYLE INVENTORY: TYPICAL DAY			
TIME	TYPICAL SCHEDULE: Who, what, where, how?	SOMETIMES A CAUSE OF ANGER? (Yes/No)	POSSIBLE ADJUSTMENTS
AM			
12:00			
1:00			
2:00			
3:00			
4:00			
5:00			
6:00			
7:00			

ENVIRONMENTAL AND LIFESTYLE INVENTORY CONT.

TIME	TYPICAL SCHEDULE: Who, what, where, how?	SOMETIMES A CAUSE OF ANGER? (Yes/No)	POSSIBLE ADJUSTMENTS
8:00			
9:00			
10:00			
11:00			
PM			
12:00			
1:00			
2:00			
3:00			

ENVIRONMENTAL AND LIFESTYLE INVENTORY CONT.			
TIME	TYPICAL SCHEDULE: Who, what, where, how?	SOMETIMES A CAUSE OF ANGER? (Yes/No)	POSSIBLE ADJUSTMENTS
4:00			
5:00			
6:00			
7:00			
8:00			
9:00			
10:00			
11:00			

• *Inventory Concluded*

PERSONAL INVENTORY: OUTLOOK ON LIFE

| Yourself/ Your World | RATE THIS ASPECT | | | | | How Can You Improve This Aspect? | How Can You Improve Your Outlook on This? |
	1 Great	2 Good	3 OK	4 Bad	5 Awful		
Your Mind	1	2	3	4	5		
Your Body	1	2	3	4	5		
Your Spirit	1	2	3	4	5		
Your Day-to-Day Learning	1	2	3	4	5		
Your Relationships	1	2	3	4	5		
Your Achievements	1	2	3	4	5		

PERSONAL INVENTORY CONT.							How Can You Improve This Aspect?	How Can You Improve Your Outlook on This?
Yourself/ Your World	RATE THIS ASPECT							
	1 Great	2 Good	3 OK	4 Bad	5 Awful			
Your Opportunities	1	2	3	4	5			
Available Information	1	2	3	4	5			
Available Food and Drink	1	2	3	4	5			
Available Shelter	1	2	3	4	5			
Opportunities to Exercise	1	2	3	4	5			
People You Know	1	2	3	4	5			

PERSONAL INVENTORY CONT.

Yourself/ Your World	RATE THIS ASPECT					How Can You Improve This Aspect?	How Can You Improve Your Outlook on This?
	1 Great	2 Good	3 OK	4 Bad	5 Awful		
Established Institutions	1	2	3	4	5		
Opportunities for Fun	1	2	3	4	5		
Your Employer	1	2	3	4	5		
Your Friends and Family	1	2	3	4	5		
Your Community	1	2	3	4	5		
People in General	1	2	3	4	5		

• Inventory Concluded

Start Taking Better Care of Yourself

Make sure you're getting enough sleep and exercise. Eat well, selecting healthy foods, but don't eat too much. Drink lots of water and less coffee and liquor. If you smoke or do drugs, stop. The better you feel physically, the less susceptible you will be to anger. Lack of sleep, health problems, alcohol consumption, and drug use all increase the likelihood that even small annoyances will provoke your anger. In the long run, feeling good physically will contribute to a healthier approach to anger and make harmful anger less likely.

That said, you also need time alone to think and relax. Schedule personal time for just *thinking*—not watching television, reading, doing chores, or anything else.

Finally, take care of yourself in your dealings with other people. Be assertive (not aggressive), expressing your needs and wants in straight, simple terms. That doesn't mean you need to become selfish and unreasonable. But if you keep your needs and wants to yourself and never express them, you're likely to be very disappointed very frequently. And that leads to resentment and anger. Other people cannot read your mind; so you have to speak up and make yourself understood.

2. Calm Yourself Physically

No matter how diligently you try to avoid anger, you will still get angry on occasion. Pay attention to the people and circumstances that tend to make you angry, and learn to recognize the early warning signs of anger:

- Do you tense up? Clench your fists?

- Does your heart race?

- Do you sweat? Flush? Pale?

- Do you breathe rapidly? Grind your teeth? Glare? Shudder? Twitch? Become speechless? Feel like yelling? Crying? Hitting?

When you detect those warning signs, take the first step to effective anger management by calming yourself down. How? Try one or more of these techniques:

Physical Exercises

— Jump up and down eight times.

— Do 11 jumping jacks.

— Clench your muscles—fists, toes, legs, arms, chest, stomach, neck, face—and release them. Do this three times.

— Close your eyes and clasp your hands behind your head and count to nine.

— Close your eyes and breathe in through your nose and out through your mouth. Do this 10 times.

— Close your eyes, cross your arms in front of you and clasp your shoulders (right shoulder with left hand, left shoulder with right hand). Hug yourself and rock from side to side five times.

— Take a five- or 10-minute walk or run.

Mental Exercises

— Close your eyes and sing or hum to yourself.

— Recite a brief poem to yourself, or say a prayer.

— Tell yourself, "Relax, don't let this get to you." Do this 10 times.

— Count backward from 100.

— Tell yourself a joke, or think of something funny.

— Think of someone you love.

— Think of a beautiful place where you've spent important time.

The physical exercises will help to dissipate or at least diffuse your anger, and the mental exercises will help to slow your heart rate and reverse some of the adjustments your body is making to prepare for aggression. These techniques will also give you enough distance— physical and/or temporal—to think through the situation and break it down into its component parts.

Note that any physically purposeful interruption (exercise or exertion) and form of mental relaxation will provide similar benefits.

3. Think Logically

It's critical to realize that what makes us angry is not just a certain stimulus but also our interpretation of that stimulus. For this reason, once you've begun to calm yourself physically, it's time to start thinking—to review your situation before you speak or act.

First, admit to yourself that you're angry and remind yourself that anger distorts your thinking; then get ready to do some cognitive restructuring. As you think through the situation, stay away from absolutes like "never" and "always." These are detrimental because:

- They are usually inaccurate.

- They make you feel overly justified in your anger.

- They suggest that a situation cannot be changed (and thus that problems cannot be solved).

- When expressed, they alienate people who might otherwise be willing to work toward a solution.

Start asking and answering these questions for yourself:

- Who or what is making me angry?

- Why am I angry?

- What provoked me? When? How?

- Is there an alternative explanation for the provoking event?

- How would the other people involved describe the provoking event?

- Does my self-esteem feel threatened?

- How do I feel? Do I feel betrayed? Disapproved of? Deprived? Exploited? Frustrated? Humiliated? Manipulated? Restricted? Threatened?

- What is my anger telling me? What data is it providing?

- Is my anger legitimate? If so, why? And at whom or what should I be directing it?

- How angry should I be under the circumstances?

- What are some reasons why I should be less angry?

- What do I want to accomplish with my anger?

Questions such as these help you develop a task orientation toward the anger, in place of an ego-driven focus. Again, admit to yourself that you're angry. Simply say, "I am angry at [OBJECT OF ANGER] because [REASON]." Then set your intentions to do the following:

- Express your feelings effectively to the appropriate recipient of your anger

- Seek solutions to the underlying cause of the anger

- Let go of the anger

4. Express Your Feelings Appropriately and Effectively

If you want to express your feelings appropriately and effectively, you first have to know how you feel, what you think, and what you need or want. This is why it's so important to think logically before you speak or act on your anger. Angry people often jump to conclusions and react in the heat of emotion. Whether you repress anger or vent it, this approach is ineffective.

If you've calmed your physical response to anger and logically thought through your anger, then you should know whom you're angry with and why. What is more, you should have a more balanced view of the situation and a diminished level of anger. Most important, you should know what you want to accomplish with your anger.

What might you decide to accomplish by *expressing* your anger? There are a number of possibilities:

- You might seek revenge for the hurt you feel.

- You might try to repair hurt feelings by confiding your vulnerability to the person who hurt you. Here you hope you'll receive an apology, an admission of the other person's vulnerability, or a similar gratifying response.

- You might remove an obstacle to effective communication by "clearing the air."

- You might seek a specific remedy to a particular, identifiable harm.

- You might look for ways to prevent similar anger-provoking events from occurring in the future.

Of course, all but the first of the above goals are productive. While the desire for revenge is a natural impulse, it is extremely counterproductive, escalating conflict, fear, defensiveness, and anger, and posing serious problems for effective resolution.

Express your anger in the right words to the right person at the right time. Schedule a meeting soon, but not too soon, to discuss the matter with the appropriate person. Remember your goal: What do you want to accomplish? Decide what you want to say. For example, "I am angry with you because [REASON]. I think the underlying cause of my anger is [CAUSE]. What I want [or need] now is [WANT OR NEED]." Be honest. Be reasonable. Keep the message brief, straight, and simple.

When you know what you want to say, rehearse. However, when you speak with the other person, remember that you want to have a conversation, not give a speech. Say up front, "I know we may have different points of view about this situation. I'd like to tell you how I feel, and I'd like to know how you feel. Would you like me to go first? I'll be very brief." When it's your turn to speak, you can present your case.

Be sure to listen carefully to the other person's viewpoint. Don't get distracted; don't start preparing defensive responses; don't interrupt. Listen. Hear what the person is saying. Perhaps he or she is still upset and expressing a lot of anger. The person might even respond vengefully, seeking to hurt you because you hurt him or her. Try to listen and realize that. If the person's response begins to make you angry, try to calm down and think logically.

As you're listening, try to identify next steps. Maintain a task orientation: You think you know the underlying cause of your anger. What is the underlying cause of the other person's anger? You know what you want or need (your goals). What does the other person need or want (what are his or her goals)? Are your goals in alignment with the person's goals, or do they clash? What is the relationship between the cause of your anger and the cause of the other person's anger?

Bear in mind, there are cases when a person's behavior or an entire situation is unacceptable. In such a case, you must be able to describe the behavior or situation, take responsibility for your view that it is unacceptable, and describe the behavior or situation and its tangible effects. If the anger's causes are intransigent or the person's goals and yours are mutually exclusive, there may be no obvious next steps. Here the best approach is negotiation—to work together to arrive at a mutually acceptable solution involving mutual compromises.

If you wish to use the data provided by anger to your advantage, you must go beyond resolving acute hostility. The next step is to seek solutions to the underlying causes of the anger.

5. Seek Solutions to the Underlying Causes of Your Anger

Remember that anger has a wide range of causes and influencing factors. Some issues can be addressed easily; others are more difficult. For example, if you're ticked off that you didn't get a free donut at work on Friday, you can come to work earlier next Friday, in plenty of time to get a donut. Or you can go buy yourself one. Or you can congratulate yourself on saving the calories. That's an easy one. More challenging would be if you were angry that you didn't get a promotion or a significant raise this year. But you can take action: build new skills, tackle important projects, do great work, and impress important decision-makers.

Other issues are simply beyond reach. For example, if you're angry at a system that allows terrorism to occur, there may not be much you can do. Still, you can seek a solution that will help your anger by changing your response to the underlying cause.

First, you must look closer at the underlying cause of your anger. By this point, you should be clear about who or what is making you angry and why. Ask and answer the following questions:

- Are you angry about some large systemic factor (the weather, the economy, the culture, the government, the company)?

- Do you perceive some inequity somewhere?

- Are your goals being blocked somehow?

- Are you clashing with someone over values?

- Are you dealing with someone who has authority over you in a formal or informal hierarchy? Is the person using that authority in a way that is making you angry?

- Are you dealing with someone who answers to you as an authority in a formal or informal hierarchy? Is the person letting you down in some way?

- Is your self-esteem being threatened in some way? How?

- Do you feel betrayed? Disapproved of? Deprived? Exploited? Frustrated? Humiliated? Manipulated? Restricted? Threatened?

Second, ask yourself: Is the underlying cause something I can change? If the answer is yes, prepare to make a plan of action. If the answer is no, prepare to make a plan of action that will help you change how you feel about the cause or at least how you respond to those feelings. In the end, you may simply have to "let it go."

Third, make your plan of action:

- State the cause of your anger.

- State your objective in the form of a concrete goal with a clear deadline.

- Schedule intermediate goals and deadlines.

- Plan your next steps. What are you going to do about this today?

- Monitor achievements along the way and stay on track.

Be aware that some plans of action take a long time to implement. If the undertaking is worthwhile, stick it out; but don't hold onto your anger. Draw strength from the fact that you're taking action to address the underlying cause, and channel your anger into that action. As for any residual anger, "let it go."

Finally, upon reflection you may decide that changing the underlying cause is possible but not worth your time and energy. In which case, once again, you may simply have to "let it go."

6. Let It Go

You must be able to let go of your anger eventually, whether the underlying cause is (a) immediately resolved, (b) resolved over a long time, (c) impossible to resolve, or (d) simply not worth the time and energy needed to resolve it. Let go of the anger, and move on.

WORKSHEET: WORKING THROUGH YOUR ANGER

Directions: Use this worksheet as necessary to work through your anger. If you are currently in an anger-provoking situation, begin to use it right away.

1. Calm yourself physically by using one or more of these:

PHYSICAL EXERCISES

■ Jump up and down eight times.

■ Do 11 jumping jacks.

■ Clench your muscles—fists, toes, legs, arms, chest, stomach, neck, face—and release them. Do this three times.

■ Close your eyes and clasp your hands behind your head and count to nine.

■ Close your eyes and breathe through your nose and out through your mouth. Do this 10 times.

■ Close your eyes, cross your arms in front of you, and clasp your shoulders (right shoulder with left hand, left shoulder with right hand). Hug yourself and rock from side to side five times.

■ Take a five- or 10-minute walk or run.

MENTAL EXERCISES

■ Close your eyes and sing or hum to yourself.

■ Recite a brief poem to yourself, or say a prayer.

■ Tell yourself, "Relax, don't let this get to you." Do this 10 times.

■ Count backward from 100.

■ Tell yourself a joke, or think of something funny.

WORKSHEET CONT.

■ Think of someone you love.

■ Think of a beautiful place where you've spent important time.

2. Think logically. Answer these questions for yourself:

■ Who or what is making me angry?

■ Why am I angry?

■ What provoked me? When? How?

■ Is there an alternative explanation for the provoking event?

■ How would the other people involved describe the provoking event?

➤

WORKSHEET CONT.

■ Does my self-esteem feel threatened?

■ How do I feel? Do I feel betrayed? Disapproved of? Deprived? Exploited? Frustrated? Humiliated? Manipulated? Restricted? Threatened?

■ What is my anger telling me? What data is it providing?

■ Is my anger legitimate? If so, why?

■ If my anger is legitimate, at whom or what should I be directing my anger?

■ How angry should I be, considering the circumstances?

WORKSHEET CONT.

■ What are some reasons why I should be less angry?

■ What do I want to accomplish with my anger?

3. Prepare to express your feelings appropriately and effectively. Decide what you want to say:

I am angry with you because:

I think the underlying cause of my anger is:

What I want [or need] right now is:

➤

WORKSHEET CONT.

4. Look closer at the underlying cause of your anger:

■ Are you angry about some large systemic factor? (E.g., the weather, economy, culture, government, company.)

■ Do you perceive some inequity somewhere?

■ Are your goals being blocked somehow?

■ Are you clashing with someone over values?

■ Are you dealing with someone who has authority over you in a formal or informal hierarchy? If so, is the person using that authority in a way that is making you angry?

■ Are you dealing with someone who answers to you as an authority in a formal or informal hierarchy? If so, is the person letting you down in some way?

WORKSHEET CONT.

■ Again, is your self-esteem being threatened in some way? If so, how?

■ Again, do you feel betrayed? Disapproved of? Deprived? Exploited? Frustrated? Humiliated? Manipulated? Restricted? Threatened?

5. Is the underlying cause something you can change? If so, make a plan of action. If not, make a plan of action that will help you change how you feel about the cause or at least how you respond to those feelings.

   ■ State the cause of your anger:

   ■ State your objective in the form of a concrete goal with a clear deadline:

WORKSHEET CONT.

■ Make a schedule of intermediate goals and deadlines:

GOALS	DEADLINES

■ Plan your next steps. What are you going to do about this *today?*

■ Monitor achievements along the way and stay on track.

ACHIEVEMENTS

6. Let go of anger.

• *Worksheet Concluded*

CHAPTER 7

Dealing With
the Angry Individual

WHILE DEALING WITH ANGER in yourself is complex
and challenging, dealing with anger in other people is a
whole new can of worms. Think about how defensive
you feel when confronting your own anger. Now think
about how threatened you feel when someone else con-
fronts your anger, telling you to "calm down," "lower
your voice," "take a timeout," or "let it go." By recall-
ing what it feels like when *you're* angry and someone
tries to engage with and manage *your* anger, you will
be in a better position to deal effectively with another
person's anger.

Dealing with one individual can be very different from
dealing with another. There are several factors to keep
in mind:

1. The individual's idiosyncrasies. Is the person
   generally approachable? Is the person anger-in
   or anger-out? Is the person aggressive? Does

the person tend to listen? Does the person have a track record of responding well to feedback?

2. Your relationship with the individual. Do you have some kind of rapport with the person? Is the person in a position of authority over you (boss, customer)? Are you in a position of authority over the other person (subordinate, vendor)? Is the person a peer?

3. The nature of the angry expression. Has the individual over-expressed his or her anger? Under-expressed it? Very effectively and appropriately expressed it?

4. The gravity of the anger. Is the person mildly irritated, furious, or somewhere in between?

5. The underlying cause. Can the cause be addressed easily? Is the cause beyond easy remedy? Can the cause be addressed at least partially? Is the cause beyond remedy entirely?

6. Your particular style. Are you outgoing? Introverted? Direct? Indirect? Confrontational? Non-confrontational?

In the workplace, you interact with many people: customers, vendors, peers, subordinates, and bosses. Any of them can become angry for any number of reasons, and it is not always your responsibility to become directly involved with that anger. Sometimes it's best to avoid engagement and let the appropriate party manage the anger. You have to make that judgment for yourself case by case, based on the circumstances. However, when the angry person is a subordinate over whom you have direct supervisory authority, *you* are the appropriate party and must take responsibility for dealing with the situation.

In many cases, anger emerges unpredictably from disruptions in work tasks or from the actions of others; thus if you as manager are present, you must react "in the moment" to the angry individual. It is highly important to avoid the three most common pitfalls here:

- Ignoring the anger

- Shutting it down through nonverbal communication that it's "not okay to express anger"

- Attempting to shout down the angry individual and "trump" his or her anger.

Instead, you must acknowledge that feeling the anger and expressing it is okay, while escalating the anger and behaving aggressively is unacceptable. You can say, "Your anger is important. The issue must be addressed. Let's talk about it in an appropriate time and place." Exhibiting calmness and a willingness to engage the employee are essential in these situations.

If the angry individual has harmed or is likely to harm others directly or indirectly, you must remove the person from the workplace at least temporarily and direct the person to professional help. In some cases, you may need to alert company security or law enforcement officials. Fortunately, situations such as this tend to be in the minority.

Five-Step Process for Managing the Angry Individual

In most cases, you can engage the angry individual appropriately and effectively, mollify the situation in the short term, and address the underlying causes in the long term. There are five basic steps to follow:

1. Start with yourself.
2. Gather information.
3. Schedule a meeting soon.
4. Engage the person.
5. Evaluate and take action.

I. Start With Yourself

Be aware of your own feelings of anger and how those feelings may affect your interactions and relationships at work. A common response when dealing with angry people is to become angry in return because of the discomfort and disruption caused by their anger. It's very helpful simply to remind yourself that you may be angry too, and to manage your own anger first.

You also should be aware that part of an employee's anger may be directed at you, even if you're not directly involved in the problem at hand. It's likely that the individual feels less in control of the situation because of your authority. If you become angry in turn, your ability to listen to the employee will be compromised and probably make the situation far worse.

2. Gather Information

Try to find out what's going on from at least two independent sources. If you cannot find the answers from independent sources, you will have to rely on the people directly involved. Bear in mind that they may have very distorted versions of the information. Don't play judge. By placing yourself in the role of "information gatherer," you will diminish the potential defensive responses of the angry individual and give yourself greater credibility to ultimately resolve the situation. Remember, when you are gathering information, you are trying to identify the underlying source of the anger.

3. Schedule a Meeting Soon

Meet with the person on the day of the incident, but not "right this moment." Let a few hours pass in between, so both of you have time to prepare for a potentially difficult conversation. Anger is exaggerated when people are distracted, stressed, or not feeling their best. Therefore, select a time when both of you can freely discuss the situation with as little distraction as possible. But don't put off the meeting to another day—that will only leave time for the anger to fester.

Be strategic about the place of the meeting as well. If you want to emphasize your authority in the situation, your office may properly convey the message of who is ultimately in control. If you'd like to emphasize your concern for the employee and convey more neutrality, select a site where you can de-emphasize your power, such as a conference room or off-site location. In most cases, if you wish to find the real cause of the anger and address it, you will want to de-emphasize your authority and try to address the employee on as equal a footing as possible. Your authority, after all, is probably not in doubt. What you need to convey is that you care about the employee and what caused his or her anger, and that you'd like to resolve the situation.

It is very important that you prepare in advance for the meeting. Question your assumptions and suspend judgment. You need to gather information. Rehearse what you are going to say and decide what you are *not* going to say. While it is critical that you listen carefully before making any judgments, it may be necessary for you, as the manager, to give the angry person feedback about the episode in question.

4. Engage the Person

When you meet with the angry individual, remember that your primary task is to listen. Let the angry person express the anger in his or her own words. Listen carefully and actively, but don't interrupt. Guide the discussion only when necessary, and use neutral but probing questions such as "How?," "Why?," and "Can you be more specific?" Try to gather more data from the anger. Throughout the meeting, exhibit respect, sensitivity, open-mindedness, flexibility, and tolerance.

Sometimes angry people simply want to vent their anger to another person—especially a person in a position of authority. If the angry individual wants to vent, remember two important facts:

- Venting anger does not relieve angry feelings and sometimes exacerbates them.
- You do not have an obligation to make yourself the recipient of undifferentiated hostility.

Make clear that the reason for the meeting is to get to the underlying cause of the anger and attempt to resolve it. Let the person vent, but only enough to convey the information. If the individual is repeating the same words again and again, raising his or her voice consistently, and speaking in absolutes like "always" and "never," then you may need to cut off the venting.

Be aware, though, that the individual may consider it a significant remedy—or at least a first step—simply to be heard on the matter by an authority figure. Often you can minimize over-venting by listening intently and *silently*. If you appear to be contemplating the individual's words, he or she will probably choose them more carefully.

While you want to focus on the individual during the meeting—making eye contact, nodding your head, showing concern, smiling when appropriate—you also want to take notes. This signals that you're taking the matter seriously and provides a record of the conversation. To add even more gravity, consider tape-recording the conversation. (Be sure to ask for permission or at least inform the individual.)

Finally, in cases where there is a lack of trust between you and the angry individual, it may be appropriate to ask a neutral third person to be present at the meeting, preferably someone who is also an authority figure. Again, your primary purpose is to listen not just for the immediate facts but also for the underlying cause of the anger.

5. Evaluate and Take Action

If there is a clear source of the anger, that source must be addressed. By now you've already taken an important step by listening to the angry individual. After listening, you must evaluate the situation:

- Is the anger legitimate?
- If so, was the individual's behavior appropriate?

These are two different questions. You should take action on both.

First, provide constructive feedback on the way the individual expressed the anger. If the person handled the situation well, you should offer positive feedback to reinforce the behavior. If the individual handled the situation in an unacceptable or inappropriate way, you must address this matter directly. Explain your expectations for behavior in similar situations. In cases where the person needs to develop anger-management skills, direct him or her to a professional or provide coaching based on the guidelines for dealing with anger in yourself (see Chapter 6).

Second, seek a solution to the underlying cause of the anger. Is there a legitimate issue that requires action? If the angry person has confided in you, explaining the source of the anger, then he or she assumes that you will try to address that problem. If you take no action, the person is apt to feel a sense of betrayal—which will only lead to more angry feelings and potentially unhealthy behavior. However, if you listen carefully, evaluate fully, and take concrete steps to address the source of the anger, you will help to assuage the anger. Equally important, you will be able to use the data from your investigation to seize opportunities for improvement. That's how you turn anger from a negative to a positive influence in your workplace.

WORKSHEET: DEALING WITH THE ANGRY INDIVIDUAL

Directions: Use this worksheet as necessary to deal with anger in other individuals. If you are currently in a problematic situation, begin to use it right away.

1. Who is the individual? What is your relationship to him or her? Describe the situation at hand.

2. Think about the individual in general. Is this person usually approachable? Is the person anger-in or anger-out? Aggressive? A good listener? Does the person have a track record of responding well to feedback?

➤

WORKSHEET CONT.

3. Are you the right person to deal with this individual's anger? Do you have some kind of rapport with him or her? Does the person have authority over you, or vice versa? Is the person a peer?

4. How do you know the person is angry? Has the person over-expressed, under-expressed, or appropriately and effectively expressed his or her anger?

5. Evaluate the status of the anger: Is the person mildly irritated, furious, or somewhere in between?

➤

WORKSHEET CONT.

6. Start with yourself. Remember:
   - Calm yourself physically.
   - Think logically.
   - Express your feelings appropriately and effectively.
   - Seek solutions to the underlying causes of your anger.
   - Let it go.

7. Gather information from at least two independent sources:

   Who is angry, and why?

   Who or what is the target of the anger?

   What happened?

   When did it happen?

   How did it happen?

8. Schedule a meeting and rehearse the following:
   - *"I think you are angry because ..."*
   - *"I want to hear your side of the story."*
   - *"Who or what made you angry, and why?"*
   - *"What happened?"*
   - *"When did it happen?"*
   - *"How did it happen?"*

   ➤

WORKSHEET CONT.

9. At the meeting, engage the person and listen carefully before making any judgments. Be sure to listen for the anger's underlying cause as well as the immediate facts.

Try to determine whether the person is angry because of one or more of the following:

- The system
- Blocked goals
- Authority-related problems
- Perceived inequity
- Clash over values
- An attack on self-esteem

- Feeling betrayed. Disapproved of. Deprived. Exploited. Frustrated. Humiliated. Manipulated. Restricted. Threatened.

10. Provide constructive feedback on the way the person expressed his or her anger.

If the person handled the situation well, offer positive feedback to reinforce the behavior. For example:

—*"I think your actions were appropriate because ..."*

—*"I want to thank you for handling the situation so well."*

—*"If something like this happens again, please handle it in the same way."*

If the person expressed anger in an unacceptable or inappropriate way, address the matter directly. For example:

—*"I think your actions were unacceptable because ..."*

—*"Your actions had these negative results ..."*

—*"If you behave this way again, I will have to impose the following penalty ..."*

—*"If you are faced with a similar situation in the future, please do the following ..."*

➤

WORKSHEET CONT.

11. Seek a solution to the underlying cause of the anger. What is the legitimate issue that requires action?

■ State your objective in the form of a concrete goal with a clear deadline:

■ Make a schedule of intermediate goals and deadlines:

GOALS	DEADLINES

■ Plan your next steps. What are you going to do about this *today?*

■ Monitor achievements along the way and stay on track.

ACHIEVEMENTS

• *Worksheet Concluded*

CHAPTER 8

Dealing With Anger in Your Organization or Team

IF YOU ARE IN A POSITION of organizational or team leadership, you should continually assess the workplace to identify its strengths and weaknesses. This should include the tracking of anger. We've discussed the high costs that an organization or a team can incur if anger is poorly managed. And we know that anger is unavoidable because the workplace involves complex relationships, high stakes, significant pressure, and many forces beyond our immediate control. While it can be difficult to manage anger in ourselves and others, dealing with anger in organizations and teams can pose our greatest challenge, especially if the anger is pervasive and derived from systemic causes.

To get an idea of the state of anger in your organization or team, complete the assessment on the next page. It will bring you a step closer to understanding what role anger is playing in your organization or team. If you find that anger is a significant problem, you must take steps to address it. If the problem rises to the level of a crisis, you may want to consider a group intervention.

✦ ASSESSMENT:

Exploring Anger in Your Organization or Team

Directions: Answer the following questions, applying them to the people in your organization or on your team. If you wish, complete the assessment twice, for your organization and team, respectively.

1. Do some people express anger directly or indirectly? If so, how often?

2. Are there particular individuals who express anger much more often than others? Do you think they are giving voice to feelings that others share, or are they in the minority?

➤

ASSESSMENT CONT.

3. Do some people become angry when they are not in control of their work situation? Who? How often? What happens?

4. Do some people become angry when they cannot control the work situations of other individuals? Who? How often? What happens?

5. Do some people become angry when they cannot have things their way? Who? How often? What happens?

➤

ASSESSMENT CONT.

6. Do some people express their anger in aggressive, inappropriate ways? Who? How often? What happens?

7. Do you think some people get angry but hide that anger behind a smiling face? Who? How often? What happens?

8. Do some people tend to hold grudges, resent others, or find ways to get even with others? Who? How often? What happens?

➤

ASSESSMENT CONT.

9. Do some people tend to blame other individuals, teams, departments, vendors, or customers when things don't work out? Who? How often? What happens?

10. Do some people scream, throw things, pout, or yell when they can't get what they want? Who? How often? What happens?

11. Do some people refuse to communicate with or work with other individuals, teams, departments, vendors, or customers? Who? How often? What happens?

➤

ASSESSMENT CONT.

12. Do some people exhibit hostility, jealousy, or sarcasm when talking about or with other individuals, teams, departments, vendors, or customers? Who? How often? What happens?

13. Do some people use absolutes like "always" and "never" when they talk about or with other individuals, teams, departments, vendors, or customers? Who? How often? What happens?

➤

ASSESSMENT CONT.

14. Do some people have formal, icy interactions with others that sometimes deteriorate into arguments? Who? How often? What happens?

15. Are there increasingly more conflicts that require arbitration or mediation from an outside party such as an authority figure? Who is involved? How often? What happens?

Considering your responses above, rate the problem of anger in your organization or team from 1 (not a problem) to 10 (an urgent crisis).

Rating:

• *Assessment Concluded*

Getting People Focused

Remember that everyone brings different skills and knowledge to the table and is capable of achieving the tasks and responsibilities required. Get things back on track and restore harmony by focusing people on their shared mission instead of on personality differences. Those who cannot focus on what is important—bringing the team's resources to bear on the mission and their particular roles and goals in relation to that mission—will not be able to continue as team members.

To set the focus, call a team meeting. Everybody must attend. You will need to accomplish three things:

1. Clear the air.

2. Clarify mission, roles, and goals.

3. Establish ground rules for conduct and for keeping communication lines open.

I. Clear the Air

Have each person take a turn speaking for three minutes. This process continues for three rounds:

- **Round 1**—The speaker says one thing that he or she appreciates about each team member.

- **Round 2**—The speaker says one thing that he or she thinks each member needs to improve.

- **Round 3**—The speaker says one thing that he

or she is committed to improving about his or her own performance or behavior.

2. Clarify Mission, Roles, and Goals

What work needs to be done by each team member? What projects, tasks, and responsibilities are involved? What deadlines and guidelines must be observed? Communicate the clear mission, goals, deadlines, and guidelines, indicating which guidelines are negotiable and which are not. Once you convey that information, see who will continue as a team member and who will not.

3. Establish Ground Rules for Conduct and for Keeping Communication Lines Open

Let people know that it's acceptable to express anger appropriately and effectively—at the right time and place to the right people in a productive, task-oriented manner. Share with people the approach to dealing with anger in yourself (see Chapter 6) and offer coaching to those who need it. Plan a follow-up meeting with the team to gauge improvements. Then get back to work.

Organizational Anger Management: Best Practices

Even if your workplace is not at the crisis stage of anger, you should be aware of the systemic factors that can create widespread anger in organizations and teams. Of course, organizations that treat people in ways that are abusive, neglectful, unethical, or illegal will incur a great deal of much-deserved wrath. But there are many perfectly standard business practices that make individuals feel undervalued, and these too are likely to cause pervasive anger. They include:

— Arbitrary policies
— Restrictive rules
— Rigid hierarchies
— Authoritarian managers
— One-way communication
— Limited information sharing
— Closed (or zero-sum) competition
— Narrow territorial boundaries
— Minimal individual autonomy
— Few rewards for good performance

In contrast, people are far less likely to become angry at their employer when they have a reasonable degree of control over their work schedules, workspace, tasks, responsibilities, learning opportunities, relationships, and compensation. Indeed, the more control an individual has over these factors, the more likely he or she is to feel very positive about an organization or team.

People also tend to place great value on two-way communication: They want a chance to contribute their input on matters that affect them directly and indirectly. What is more, they want to receive recognition and rewards when they make valuable contributions.

While organization-wide practices can have a huge impact on anger in the workplace, the most powerful factor is the relationship between managers and their direct reports. When managers are highly informed, engaged, and responsive, they tend to have relationships of trust and confidence with their direct reports.

However, a well-run organization with good managers may still have pervasive problems with anger. Therefore, the following anger-management best practices must also be implemented:

1. Establish clear expectations for workplace behavior.

2. Require leaders and managers to model appropriate behavior.

3. Do not select or promote people who fail to manage their own anger.

4. Provide resources for anger management and confront dangerous anger early on.

I. Establish Clear Expectations for Workplace Behavior

Managers should make clear their expectations of how people will conduct themselves in the workplace. Angry expressions that demean others should be strictly forbidden. Some companies, including Polaroid, Nordstrom, General Electric, and Quaker Oats, list among their core values specific forms of interpersonal conduct among employees. For example, they explicitly state that intimidation and hostile or offensive behavior will not be condoned (see Pearson, Andersson, and Porath, 2000). When expectations are established and well known, the clear inappropriateness of behavior that violates these expectations sets the ground for corrective action.

2. Require Leaders and Managers to Model Appropriate Behavior

As discussed earlier, anger in hierarchies tends to move downward. When leaders demonstrate their anger by yelling and screaming, these behaviors are repeated down to the lowest levels, creating a reinforcing cycle of anger on the part of superiors and fear on the part of subordinates. Moreover, those who use their anger inappropriately tend to use their power to silence those who are below them and who might raise questions.

Since employees scrutinize their leaders' behavior for signals of appropriate and acceptable conduct, leaders who value respect among employees must also manage their own expressions of anger. They should be models of what is appropriate in terms of anger, avoiding aggression. The authority held by superiors confers the responsibility of supporting, coaching, and empowering others, not the right to dominate them. It also confers the responsibility of penalizing those who harm others through aggression.

3. Do Not Select or Promote People Who Fail to Manage Their Own Anger

Some people are actually known for their bad tempers —they leave a trail of casualties behind them wherever they work. Yet they get hired and promoted again and again. Why is that? Often organizations hire and promote people on the sole basis of financial or technical performance. Although such performance is certainly valuable, this value is outweighed by the damage inflicted on individuals, teams, and organizations when these people, especially those in positions of authority, express their anger aggressively and repeatedly.

Thus, when you select individuals for open positions or for promotions, it is critical to evaluate their skills and track record on interpersonal communication. Selection criteria and performance evaluations should give considerable weight to such skills and the ability to build work-group morale. Reward individuals who excel in these areas, and penalize those who indulge their tempers at the expense of the organization.

4. Provide Resources for Anger Management and Confront Dangerous Anger Early On

Everyone in the workplace feels anger sometimes and must deal with it. Provide self-study materials that help individuals learn how to manage their own anger.

In addition, provide managers with training in conflict resolution, negotiation, and coaching. They must be brave enough to intervene in extreme cases, and should know how to do the following:

- Confront the problem employee

- Offer help and support if appropriate

- Remove the employee from the workplace and notify potential targets, company security, and law enforcement officials

In less extreme cases, when chronic anger is a problem for an otherwise valuable employee, managers should encourage or require the person to seek professional help. Too often, managers try to avoid angry employees because the anger makes them feel uncomfortable or afraid. They may even move the problem employee along to another part of the firm. Of course, these defensive reactions do not solve the problem, but leave it to fester.

What is the state of the four best practices in your organization or team? What possible adjustments could be made? What next steps could be taken? Use the worksheet on the following page to tackle these questions.

WORKSHEET: MOVING TOWARD BEST PRACTICES

DIRECTIONS: What is the current state of each best practice in your organization or team? What adjustments could be made? What are your next steps?

BEST PRACTICE	CURRENT STATE	POSSIBLE ADJUSTMENTS	NEXT STEPS
1. Establish clear expectations for workplace behavior.			
2. Require leaders and managers to model appropriate behavior.			

WORKSHEET CONT.			
BEST PRACTICE	**CURRENT STATE**	**POSSIBLE ADJUSTMENTS**	**NEXT STEPS**
3. Do not select or promote people who fail to manage their own anger.			
4. Provide resources for anger management and confront dangerous anger early on.			

• Worksheet Concluded

In Conclusion . . .

THE COSTS OF ANGER in the workplace can be great, but so can the benefits. Whenever you diagnose anger as an issue for you, another individual, your team, or your organization, you must be prepared to take action. With that in mind, let us briefly review the main points of managing anger.

As we have seen, anger's causes may vary from person to person, but the common denominator is often interpersonal dynamics: relationships between and among people. All of us have a basic need for self-esteem—to feel valued by others and to value ourselves. Anger is driven by emotions that signal an attack on self-esteem, such as feelings of betrayal, disapproval, deprivation, exploitation, frustration, humiliation, manipulation, restriction, and threat. These emotions can be traced to any of a wide range of causes. In terms of the workplace, these causes tend to fall into five troublesome areas: (1) anger at the system, (2) perceived inequity,

(3) blocked goals, (4) divergent values, and (5) unequal power.

To manage anger effectively, you must first become more aware of your own anger. That means exploring several issues: whether you have a tendency towards anger; what kinds of things make you angry; how angry you generally become; and how you typically deal with your anger.

The next step is managing your anger by following our recommended six-step process: (1) avoid anger, (2) calm yourself physically, (3) think logically, (4) express your feelings appropriately and effectively, (5) seek solutions to the underlying causes of your anger, and (6) let it go. This is a powerful method to use for managing your anger and for coaching angry individuals on managing their anger.

Dealing with angry individuals is particularly challenging, for every individual is different. In the workplace, you interact with many people, and it is not always appropriate for you to engage the angry person directly. However, if you have direct supervisory authority over the person, you have an obligation to deal with the situation.

Be sure to engage the angry individual appropriately and effectively, try to mollify the situation in the short term, and address the underlying causes in the long term. Remember to follow these five recommended steps: (1) start with yourself, (2) gather information, (3) schedule a meeting soon (and preferably on neutral ground), (4) engage the angry person, and (5) evaluate and take action.

Finally, we encourage you to evaluate your organization or team—or both. Anger in the workplace may be unavoidable, but you can take steps to make it less pervasive and less intense. We have recommended these anger-management best practices: (1) establish clear expectations for workplace behavior, (2) require leaders and managers to model appropriate behavior, (3) do not select or promote people who fail to manage their own anger, and (4) provide resources for anger management and confront dangerous anger early on.

With great hope for the future, we wish you strength and focus in managing anger in the workplace.

References

Neuman, J. H., and Baron, R. A. 1997. Aggression in the workplace. In *Anti-social behavior in organizations,* edited by R. Giacalone and J. Greenburg. Thousand Oaks, CA: Sage.

Pearson, C., Andersson, L., and Porath, C. 2000. Assessing and attacking workplace incivility. *Organizational Dynamics,* Fall, 123–137.